ENGLISH FOR ACADEMICS

Svetlana Bogolepova
Vasiliy Gorbachev
Olga Groza
Anisya Ivanova
Lyudmila Kuznetsova
Tamara Oschepkova
Irina Pervukhina
Ekaterina Shadrova
Svetlana Suchkova

Project consultant: Rod Bolitho

A communication skills course for tutors, lecturers and PhD students

In collaboration with the British Council

BRITISH COUNCIL

BOOK 2

CAMBRIDGE UNIVERSITY PRESS

CAMBRIDGE
UNIVERSITY PRESS

University Printing House, Cambridge CB2 8BS, United Kingdom

Cambridge University Press is part of the University of Cambridge.

It furthers the University's mission by disseminating knowledge in the pursuit of education, learning and research at the highest international levels of excellence.

www.cambridge.org
Information on this title: www.cambridge.org/9781107435025

First published 2015

Printed in Dubai by Oriental Press

A catalogue record for this publication is available from the British Library

ISBN 978-1-10743502-5 Book with online audio

Additional resources for this publication at www.cambridge.org/elt/english-for-academics

Contents

Introduction

Did you know that most communication in English around the world takes place between non-native speakers using English as a *lingua franca*? This is very often the case when academics communicate with each other within their specialisms.

If you are attending classes to improve your English in order to take part in international communication in your academic field, this coursebook is intended for you. It is the second in a two-part series and deals with topics and situations that you will find relevant and helpful, within these three broad areas:

- planning and taking part in international conferences and other academic events
- writing up your research for publication in international journals
- planning and delivering your teaching through the medium of English

To get started, you will need to have an intermediate level of English (equivalent to B1+ or B2 on the Common European Framework of Reference). In class time you will be involved in challenging tasks and interesting activities together with your fellow learners. But please remember that you will also need to make time to work outside class hours in order to make significant progress in English. In this way you will build both your competence and your confidence in using English in international academic contexts.

Be ready to experiment with your English. It doesn't matter if you make some mistakes – nobody is perfect!

Module 1

Organising and participating in academic events

In this module you will:

- develop your abilities to plan, participate in and manage academic events

Unit 1 Planning a conference

By the end of this unit you will be able to
- create a timeline for planning a conference
- discuss and come to an agreement about a theme, a title and submission guidelines for a conference
- write a call for papers
- talk about different presentation formats and past conference experiences

Lesson 1 A conference planning timeline

Lead-in

1 Work in pairs. Answer the questions and make some notes. Be ready to report your answers to the whole class.

1 When did you last attend a conference?
2 What were the good and bad points in your experience of that conference?

Listening

2 2 Listen and match the conversations (1–6) with what the speaker says (a–f).

Conversation	
1	
2	
3	
4	
5	
6	

a He/She is disappointed because the actual speakers were different from those stated in the programme.
b He/She is dissatisfied with the sessions he/she attended.
c He/She likes the accommodation he/she is staying in.
d He/She is upset because it took him/her a long time to find the room he/she was presenting in.
e He/She finds the technical facilities very good.
f He/She liked the extra activities offered during the conference.

3 Work in pairs. Use the ideas from Activities 1 and 2 and make a list of things conference organisers should deal with in order to make a conference successful. Be ready to share your list with the whole class.

Reading

4 Read the stages of preparation for a conference (a–g) below and put them in the correct sequence.

1	2	3	4	5	6	7

Careful planning and organisation is the key to a successful conference. If you plan to host a conference, make sure the pre-conference planning period is long enough, or at least that you take into account all the stages listed below.

a

The third step will be choosing a theme and coming up with attractive objectives and a catchy title for your event. Hold a brainstorming session with your colleagues. Several heads are better than one!

b

At last, it is time to go public. Issue the call for papers. For a regional conference, you might prefer to send out two mailings: a flyer announcing the conference and the information pack containing the registration forms. Consider whether there will be on-site registration and when the deadline for cancellations is. Think about sending confirmation letters to registered participants.

c

Secondly, choose an appropriate date. Avoid dates during sporting events such as football games. Also, be aware of the winter break, mid-terms and finals. Check the calendar for major religious events and other holidays. Make a conference planning timeline and a checklist to help you to work on a day-to day basis throughout the organisation process.

d

Then, choose the venue and facilities. Find out if people can easily get to the location. It is also useful to know what other events are happening within the building that might detract from the conference. Find out if technical facilities and catering can be provided.

e

Firstly, consider your audience. When determining who your audience will be, approach some people you see as potential participants and elicit from them what types of issues, topics and programmes would be of interest to them. See it also as a good time to estimate the likely number of participants.

f

After the facilities have been chosen, start planning the programme. Decide what kind of and how many sessions you have time to offer. Prioritise to determine which topics would be better received and well attended. Nominate and contact facilitators.

g

Now you have a theme, it is time to establish a budget. Make a checklist of everything you will need – resources, rental, payments to support staff, catering, publicity material, conference programme, postage, speakers' expenses etc. Once you have arrived at a figure, you may need to approach potential sponsors to provide some of the finance you need. This budgeting exercise will also help you to set a registration fee for participants. This should be done at an early stage.

5 Use the text in Activity 4 to fill in the table about the stages of preparation for a conference. Use only key words and/or short phrases.

Stages	Things to consider	How to complete the stages
1 *Determine the audience*	*Types of interesting issues, topics, programmes, conference attendance*	*Approach potential participants, elicit types of issues, topics, programmes*
2		
3		
4		
5		
6		
7		

6 Compare your notes in pairs and add to them if something important is missing.

Language focus

7 Match the verbs (1–7) with their objects (a–g) and check your answers by referring to the text in Activity 4.

1 to host
2 to offer
3 to nominate
4 to approach
5 to set
6 to receive
7 to make

a a checklist
b someone for financial support
c a conference
d a topic
e a session
f a registration fee
g facilitators

8 Use the phrases from Activity 7 to complete the sentences below. Change the form and word order if necessary. Use each phrase only once.

1 Now, as we have decided on the list of events, let's move on to ______________ for them.
2 As you all know, the Siberian Federal University is ______________ on March 29th, aimed at discussing the problem of interdisciplinary studies in undergraduate programmes.
3 I suppose we could ______________ on the economic aspects of blended learning within the framework of interdisciplinary studies.
4 I think we could ______________ the Regional Education Department for ______________.
5 I'm sure this ______________ will ______________ well by the potential audience.
6 We need to ______________ that will cover our costs but is also affordable.
7 I suggest we ______________ of things to do before issuing a conference announcement.

9 You are going to take part in a planning meeting for a conference. Use your completed table in Activity 5 to write questions for this meeting.

Action Plan Meeting Agenda

Meeting information

Objective: To develop an action plan

Date:

Time:

Location:

Agenda item	Questions to discuss
1 Audience	**a** types of issues / interesting e.g. *What types of issues would be interesting to the audience?* **b** people / attend e.g. *How many people are going to attend?*
2 Dates	**c** other events / happen / at the same time
3 Title	**d** theme and objectives / attractive **e** title / catchy
4 Financial support	**f** resources / need **g** potential sponsors / approach **h** registration fee / charge
5 Venue and facilities	**i** people / get to the location **j** other events / happen / in the building **k** technical facilities and catering / available
6 Programme	**l** sessions / offer **m** topics / better received by the audience **n** facilitators / be
7 Going public	**o** mailings / send out **p** on-site registration / there be

Speaking

10 Match expressions a–j with their functions 1–7.

a You know, that's exactly what I think.
b Let's hear what (*name*) has to say.
c I'm afraid I can't agree with you there.
d I'm absolutely certain …
e All in all, we think that …
f It will probably be …
g It's impossible …
h Are you sure …?
i You are certainly right.
j I'm not sure we'll be able to …

Language Support: discussions

1 Expressing certainty ______
2 Expressing probability ______
3 Expressing doubt ______
4 Expressing agreement ______
5 Expressing disagreement ______
6 Inviting someone to contribute to a discussion ______
7 Summing up ______

11 **Work in groups of three. Complete the conversation with phrases from Activity 10 and act it out.**

Catering facilities will be available between the 2nd and 7th of April.

A: (Express certainty.)
_______________ catering facilities will be available between the 2nd and 7th of April.
B: (Express doubt.)
_______________ Isn't the folk festival scheduled for the same week?
(Invite C to contribute to the discussion.)
____
C: (Express probability.)
They normally hold the folk festival in early April so _______________ in that week.
A: (Agree/disagree.)

12 **In groups of three, develop the statements below into exchanges of opinions as in Activity 11. Use phrases from Activity 10. Act the conversations out.**

1 Early February is a good time for a conference.
2 The issue of plagiarism will be of interest for both teachers and researchers.
3 The Regional Ministry for Science and Education should be approached for sponsorship.

13 **Work in groups of five or six. Your university is going to host an international conference on using technology for teaching undergraduate courses. Hold a planning meeting. Follow the steps below.**

1 Appoint a chairperson. Assign questions from the agenda (in Activity 9) to other members of the group.
2 Spend five minutes preparing for the meeting. Follow the instructions below. Use the language you learned in Activities 5, 7 and 10.

Chairperson: Think about what you are going to say when opening the meeting. Learn the phrases you might need during the discussion (see Activity 10). Be ready to sum up at the end what you have all agreed.

Participants: Prepare your suggestions. Be ready to respond to your colleagues' suggestions. Use the phrases you learned in Activity 10.

3 Discuss each item on the agenda (in Activity 9).
4 Listen to the chairperson summarising what has been agreed. If you disagree, politely offer your opinion.

Follow-up

14 **Read about conference planning timelines and answer the questions.**

1 What is a conference planning timeline, according to the text?
2 When creating this type of timeline, what does the author suggest starting with?
3 What technique is recommended to deal with especially important dates?

An effective conference or event planning timeline will keep everyone on track and ensure you do not miss any important deadlines. An event planning timeline is not just a long to-do list, it is also a schedule of key tasks and dates that is clearly defined and easy to use.

Start with the date of your event, and work backwards, assessing how long each task will take. As early as possible, get deadlines and due dates from venues and other suppliers, and incorporate them into your timeline. You can base other tasks around these dates.

Mark on your timeline the date when the call for papers is going to be issued. If you want to have a flyer, allow time for it to be printed. Don't forget about registration deadlines for speakers and delegates. Also, make a note of the date by which applicants will be informed if their proposals have been accepted or not. It is also necessary to fix the date when the conference programme will be sent to the participants.

Consider highlighting or colour-coding urgent or non-negotiable deadlines in your timeline to make them stand out from the others.

15 **Develop a conference planning timeline based on your decisions in the simulation in Activity 13. You can work alone or in pairs or small groups. Bring your completed timeline to your next lesson.**

CONFERENCE PLANNING TIMELINE

Task	Start date	Completion date
1	… weeks before the conference	… weeks before the conference
2		
3		
4		
5		
6		
7		
8		
9		
10		

Lesson 2 A call for papers

Lead-in

1 **Look through the list of items that are normally included in a call for papers and tick the ones that are important for you. Compare your answers with other people's.**

☐ keynote speakers	☐ registration fee	☐ programme committee
☐ website	☐ submission guidelines	☐ deadlines
☐ presentation formats	☐ sponsorship	☐ conference title
☐ venue	☐ conference dates	☐ subthemes
☐ contact details	☐ selection criteria	☐ working languages

Reading

2 **Read this call for papers. Which items from the list in Activity 1 are mentioned in it?**

ASSOCIATION OF EDUCATIONAL PHILOSOPHERS

The 14th Biennial International Conference
'Old and New Generations in the 21st Century: The Shifting Landscape of Education' will take place at McLaughlin University (London), August 20th–23rd, 2016

CALL FOR PAPERS AND PRESENTATIONS

Papers are invited for the 14th Biennial International Conference of the Association of Educational Philosophers.

Conference papers and discussions will be organised around the following subthemes:

- Authority and responsibility in teacher–student relationships today
- The 21st-century school and university as sites for democracy
- The impact of new technologies on teaching and learning
- Changing conceptions of youth and adulthood
- Shifting boundaries between public and private sectors of education
- Education, childrearing and the search for a common world

PROGRAMME FORMAT

There will be three plenary sessions:
The lecture in honour of the past Association President will be given by **Robert Hughes** (University of Glasgow, UK). The two other invited speakers are **Angela Thompson** (University of Halle, Germany) and **Michele Cosenza** (University of Macerata, Italy).

In addition, there will be three types of sessions for which contributions are invited:
1) Presentations of a completed piece of research or research in progress. Each presenter is allotted 15 minutes for presenting, followed by 10 minutes for discussion, moderated by a chairperson.
2) Poster presentations. The poster (A0 format: 841 mm x 1189 mm) provides a visual presentation of the conducted research. There are 20 minutes for presenting, followed by 30 minutes of discussion, moderated by a chairperson.
3) Round tables, in which three or four participants present related papers around a particular theme. Presenters explain their research issue, and participants are invited to discuss this issue.

SUBMISSION OF PROPOSALS

Submissions should not include papers that have been published previously, presented at other conferences, or that are scheduled for other forthcoming conferences. Submissions must be no more than 2,500 words and should be prepared in accordance with the Research Paper Template. All conference proposals should be sent to the Programme Committee by **February 1st, 2016**. Proposals will be reviewed by the Conference Programme Committee. Decisions will be announced by **March 15th, 2016**. The text of the papers will be included in the *Conference Proceedings*, a hard copy of which will be available at the conference. Detailed submission guidelines are provided at www.conf2016.aep/info

The registration fee (£90) includes a hard copy of the *Conference Proceedings*, all lunches, refreshments during coffee breaks and one conference dinner.

3 **Work in pairs. Discuss the questions below and be ready to share your ideas with the whole class.**

- Would you like to contribute to this conference? Why? / Why not?
- What features make a call for papers attractive to the target audience?

Language focus

4 **Look at the diagram of a conference theme and answer the questions.**

1 Would this theme interest you and your colleagues? Why? / Why not?
2 What subthemes would you add to make it more attractive for you?

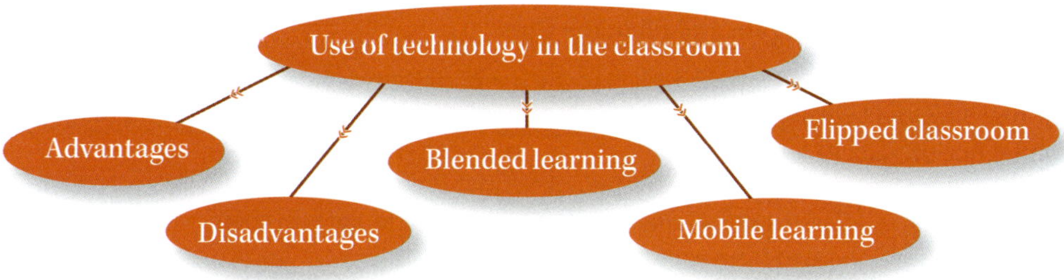

5 **Work in pairs. Choose a theme from the list below and make a diagram (as in Activity 4) for it. You can add your own theme to the list and work on it.**

- Methods of research
- Different approaches to assessment
- Interdisciplinary education
- How to share research internationally
- How to develop students' research skills
- Your own theme

6 **Present your conference diagram from Activity 5 to your colleagues. Explain why you have chosen it, using as many of the adjective–noun phrases in the table below as possible.**

	problem	topic	theme	area	field	question	issue
a common	✓	✓	✓			✓	
a critical	✓	✓	✓	✓		✓	✓
a broad		✓	✓	✓	✓	✓	
the central	✓	✓	✓			✓	✓
a/the key		✓	✓	✓		✓	✓
the main	✓	✓	✓	✓		✓	✓
a major	✓	✓	✓	✓		✓	✓
a controversial		✓	✓	✓	✓	✓	✓
a sensitive		✓	✓	✓		✓	✓
a current		✓					✓

Environmental protection is a very broad theme. It includes numerous controversial areas of research, such as the reintroduction of endangered species.

Sex education and birth control are very sensitive topics that should be dealt with carefully.

Listening

7 ⊙3 **Listen to five short conversations that occurred while planning a conference and tick the functions you hear in each conversation.**

Function	Conversation				
	1	2	3	4	5
Expressing an opinion					
Asking for more detail					
Disagreeing politely					

8 ⊙3 **Listen to the conversations again and fill in the gaps.**

1 Could you ______________ and details of the use of mobile devices in the classroom for teaching and learning purposes?
2 As for the conference theme, ______________ research than teaching methods.
3 I ______________. Getting students involved in research as early in their career as possible is central to further progress in research methodology.
4 I ______________ choose 'Sharpen Your Axe – Get the Professional Edge!' It's sure to attract attention.
5 That ______________, but to be honest, it doesn't give any idea of what the event is about.
6 Now, we have to choose an appropriate date. I ______________ November 20th because no major sports events are scheduled on that day.
7 But ______________ our music festival is planned for that date.
8 The point about gathering financial support. Could you explain it ______________?

9 **Add expressions from Activity 8 to the Language Support boxes.**

Language Support: expressing and supporting an opinion

It occurs to me that this topic is relevant for the following reasons ...
I find the topic of interest because ...

Language Support: asking for more detail

Can you be more specific about ... ?
It would be good if you could fill in some detail about ...

Language Support: disagreeing politely

I'm afraid I have to disagree on the point ...
I understand what you mean, but I really believe that ...

Speaking

10 Look at these conference titles (1–7) and say which criteria in the list below (a–d) they meet.

1 Old and New Generations in the 21st Century: The Shifting Landscape of Education
2 Quality in Higher Education
3 E-merging Forum: Bringing Together Teachers of English
4 New Trends in Education and Their Implications
5 Rivers of Language – Rivers of Learning
6 Symmetry Breaking and Pattern Formation
7 TLE for ELT

A conference title should
a give enough information on the theme
b be appealing to the target audience
c be attention-grabbing
d be clear and concise

11 Work in pairs. Think of a title for your conference. Follow the tips below.

1 Look again at the diagrams you drew in Activity 5.
2 Brainstorm possible titles.
3 Discuss each title. Use the criteria listed in Activity 10.
4 While discussing each title, follow the flow chart below and use the Language Support boxes in Activity 9.

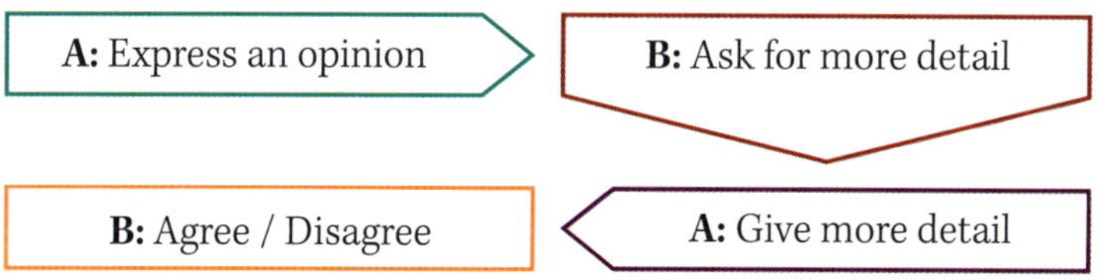

Writing

12 Look at the highlighted phrases in the text in Activity 2. What grammar structure is used in them? Find other examples in the text. Why is this structure used in the text?

13 Work in pairs. Write submission guidelines for your conference (see Activity 11). Use the text in Activity 2 for help and the plan below.

Submission Guidelines

All papers should be prepared and submitted according to the following guidelines:

1 Topics:
2 Presentation formats:
3 Length:
4 Information about the author:
5 Selection criteria:
6 Deadlines:
7 Other requirements:

Follow-up

14 Work in pairs. Produce a complete call for papers for the conference you have decided on in Activity 5. Follow the steps below.

1 If appropriate, start a blog (see www.blogger.com) or use any other way of electronic communication to discuss your document.
2 Use the example in Activity 2.
3 Send your document to your colleagues for peer evaluation.
4 Evaluate your colleagues' calls for papers. Use the checklist below:
  a The aim and the theme are clear.
  b Potential contributors can understand what they can submit, when and how to do it.
  c Information about presentation formats is provided.
  d It is clear who can be contacted if the participant has further questions.
5 If necessary, improve your document following the feedback you have received.
6 Submit your document to your teacher for assessment and feedback.

Lesson 3 Presentation formats

Lead-in

1 **Work in pairs. Look at the table about presentation formats. In each of columns 2–6, two pieces of information are in the wrong place. Use your experience of academic conferences to find and correct them.**

1	2	3	4	5	6
Presentation format	**How many speakers are there?**	**What is the focus?**	**How large is the audience?**	**What visuals are used, if any?**	**Other features**
Plenary session	All participants	The presenter's views on a broad topic	15–30	A PowerPoint presentation	It is given by a notable expert
Workshop	1 or 2	A summary of a research project	All the participants at an event	A PowerPoint presentation, handouts	It is interactive
Round-table discussion	Usually 1	A specific topic	15–30	Usually none	Short presentations are followed by a discussion
Panel discussion	2–5	Different speakers' views on a specific topic	Any	A poster	Participants are on equal terms
Poster presentation	1	Experiencing and discussing	Any	Usually none, possibly a PowerPoint presentation	Members of the audience read the poster and ask questions, the presenter answers

Listening

2 ⊙4 **Listen to the first part of a conversation about workshops. Write *T* if the statements below are true according to the speakers, *F* if they are false and *NS* if it is not stated.**

1 Josie (the first speaker) enjoys attending workshops.
2 Josie is going to facilitate a workshop.
3 According to Sarah, a workshop needs to be well planned.
4 Sarah thinks that the workshop format is useful for everybody who is involved.
5 Sarah is a very experienced facilitator.
6 According to Sarah, a good workshop can help to generate new ideas.
7 The workshop Sarah attended in Madrid helped her to establish important contacts.
8 Josie doesn't feel very confident about the workshop topic.
9 Both speakers agree that the main challenge for a workshop facilitator is to involve all participants.

3 5 **Listen to the second part of the conversation and complete the diagrams below. Compare your notes in pairs and add the missing information.**

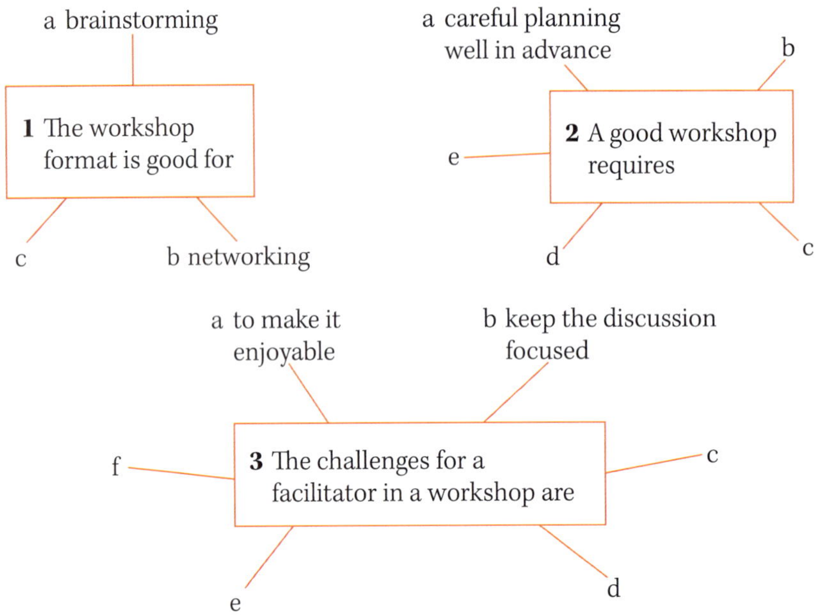

Language focus

4 **Work in pairs. Read the extracts from Alan's description of his workshop and answer the questions about the numbered parts. Report your answers to your colleagues.**

> … My first experience with facilitating workshops? Oh, it was a complete disaster. [1]Want to hear? OK. I had gathered that planning a workshop was a serious job. So, of course, I had put a lot of careful planning and creativity into it.
>
> Unfortunately, the workshop had been over-publicised. [2]Instead of the 10 to 15 attendees I had estimated, about 40 turned up! Oh, I thought, OK, I'll manage somehow … I'll split them into smaller groups for discussion! But as the attendance had exceeded expectations they had to move the workshop to a bigger room, which had columns blocking the view for part of the audience.
>
> [3]So, I failed to create an appropriate atmosphere. As a result, some people were too nervous to speak up in an unfamiliar group. I also failed to mix people up properly. So, people in the small groups were from the same institutions. They had nothing new to share!
>
> To crown it all, the workshop was scheduled for after lunch. [4]As you know, for many people, it's the least productive time of day.
>
> And finally, as often happens, there was one participant who first complimented me on my publications and then kept asking questions and interrupting me … He was very well-meaning, but … [5]I felt I was losing control! The other attendees … I could see they were losing interest. [6]So, I decided to take back control – I stood up and talked for almost an hour. After the ordeal was over, a participant came up to me. 'Thank you for this most interesting lecture, Professor,' she said. 'Anyway, how do you propose to solve the problem?'

1. What is special about sentence 1? Is it acceptable?
2. Why are different verb forms used in sentence 2? Find more examples of this kind in the extracts.
3. Why is only the past simple used in sentence 3 and the four sentences after it?
4. Why is the present simple used in sentence 4?
5. Why are *felt* (the past simple) and *was losing* (the past continuous) used in sentence 5?
6. Why is the past simple used in sentence 6, not the past continuous as in sentence 5?

5 Choose the right option to complete these statements about the use of tenses in a story about past experiences.

1 We use the *past perfect / past simple* tense when it is important to show that one of the past actions happened before the other.
2 When several actions happened at the same period of time in the past we use the *past perfect / past simple* for all the verbs.
3 When we describe a completed action in the past, we use the *past continuous / past simple.*
4 When we describe an action that happened over a period of time and was not complete, we use the *past continuous / past simple.*

6 Put the verbs in brackets in the correct form.

It's important that panellists [1]__________ (*have*) a clear picture of how the discussion will go. Once I [2]__________ (*happen*) to attend a panel discussion which [3]__________ (*turn out*) to be a complete disaster just because the panellists [4]__________ (*receive*) conflicting instructions. Three out of the four panellists [5]__________ (*arrive*) with their slide shows. Only one of them [6]__________ (*prepare*) answers for questions. When that one person [7]__________ (*answer*) the first question, the next panellist [8]__________ (*ask*) to start her slide show. While she [9]__________ (*look for*) the slide she [10]__________ (*need*) the other two panellists had to take the questions. But they also [11]__________ (*rely*) on slides, so everybody was unhappy and embarrassed.

Speaking

7 Work in small groups. Discuss the questions below and report your answers to your colleagues.

1 How are the presentation formats in the table below similar? How do they differ?

Presentation format	Plenary session	Workshop	Round-table discussion	Panel discussion
Roles	Chairperson		Moderator	

2 Participants have to accept certain roles in these formats. What are they? Complete the table.
3 Which roles are similar?
4 Which roles do you think are the most challenging? Why?

8 Find phrases in 1–9 that perform the functions in the list on the right and write them under the appropriate heading.

1 I don't think we have enough interactive events on the programme. What do you think?
2 Why don't we have a workshop on blended teaching materials?
3 If we want people to change their practices, we need them to start practising. I would go for a workshop on blended teaching materials. Are you following me?
4 I see what you mean, but a workshop requires careful planning well in advance.
5 We could change a workshop on blended teaching materials for a round-table discussion.
6 We should definitely have a workshop on blended teaching materials.
7 It occurs to me that we won't be able to give a workshop as it requires a lot of creativity and careful planning. Does that make sense?
8 To me a workshop is the best format if we are really aiming at improving teaching practices.
9 I see your point. I agree we need to nominate a facilitator as soon as possible.

Expressing an opinion

____
____
____
____

Conceding a point

____
____

Making a suggestion

____
____

Checking understanding.

____
____

9 Work in pairs. Look again at the call for papers you produced in Activity 14 in Lesson 2 (see page 18). Add or exclude some presentation formats, or decide to leave them as they are. Follow the flow chart below.

A: Express an opinion and give reasons → **B:** Support./Disagree. → **A:** Make a suggestion and check understanding. → **B:** Agree.

Follow-up

10 Answer the questions about your experience of participating in various conference events. Be ready to share your answers with the whole class.

1 What presentation formats have you experience of using?
2 Were you happy with the outcomes? Why? / Why not?
3 How did you prepare?
4 What happened on the actual day of the event?
5 What lessons have you learned?

Unit 2 Q&A sessions

By the end of this unit you will be able to
- ask a presenter different types of questions
- respond to questions and comments using various strategies
- paraphrase questions
- summarise a speaker's ideas

Lesson 1 Asking questions

Lead-in

1 **Work in pairs. Look at the cartoon. What is its message? Do you agree with it?**

2 **Work in pairs. Discuss the questions.**

1 Have you ever taken part in a Q&A session?
2 Were you the presenter or were you in the audience?
3 Was it a success? Why? / Why not?

Listening

3 6 **Listen to a summary of a presentation about activities that you can plan with digital devices. Cross out the activity which is NOT mentioned by the speaker.**

- practising content (maths, facts, spelling, etc.)
- accessing materials in different forms and sources
- assessing learners' performance
- producing joint work
- performing creative tasks

4 7 **Listen to these comments and questions from participants after the presentation. Which do you think the presenter found easiest to deal with and which were the most difficult? Why?**

5 **Match the types of questions and comments (1–4) with their descriptions (a–d).**

1 wandering statement
2 clarifying question
3 probing question
4 irrelevant question

a a question to find out more detail by asking the presenter to go deeper and explain some background behind the theory
b a question which is not connected with the topic of the talk
c a question to check a concept, to make some point from the presentation clear or easier to understand
d a speech on the topic from one of the participants

6 ⦿7 **Listen again to the questions and comments and identify their types.**

Language focus

7 **Match the sentences in the box (1–3) with the elements of a good question (a–c).**

> [1]Thank you for this very interesting presentation and sharing your experience. [2]You stated that the BYOD approach enhances learning results. [3]What evidence is there to support that?
>
> **1** ______ **2** ______ **3** ______

a the question
b acknowledgement (a kind remark that shows respect to the speaker to whom you are directing your question)
c context (clarification for the speaker and the audience members what your question is regarding)

8 **Read these examples of good questions and identify the elements listed in Activity 7.**

1 I appreciate your analysis of global trends in teachers' professional development. I fully agree with you that teachers have to talk less and teach less and give their students more opportunities to interact with each other. But I wonder how we convert our teachers into facilitators instead of taking on this role of always being at the front of the classroom. I have some ideas but I'd be interested in yours.
2 That was a very interesting presentation. You were talking earlier about the importance of needs analysis. Can you give me an example of the online tools that you used to survey the students in your target group?
3 Your presentation has started me thinking. You mentioned that only 10% of researchers in your country have publications in international scientific journals. Do you believe that the top-down methods that you are trying to implement would be the best way to guarantee positive changes?

9 In Activities 7 and 8, find phrases for each element of a good question and add them to the Language Support box.

> **Language Support: asking a good question**
> Acknowledgement: I would like to thank you for ...
>
> Context: In your talk you described ...
>
> Question: Could you specify ...?

10 Put the words in the correct order to make questions.

1 is / attitude to / What / blended learning? / your

2 if / wanted / research. / you / I / enough funding for / get / this kind of / to ask

3 your partners / institutions / Which / in / project? / were / this

4 see / your initiative? / the future / do / of / you / How

5 'flipped classroom'. / mean by / I'd like to / the term / what / to explain / you / ask you

6 to / this approach / subject area? / apply / you / any / Can

7 wonder if / conducted / provide / you / you / how / could / I / your needs analysis. / more details about

11 Read the questions in Activity 10 again and identify which questions are direct and which are indirect.

12 Compare these two questions. How does the structure of the questions differ? Which is more polite?

- What evidence is there to support that?
- Could you tell me what evidence there is to support that?

> **Language Support: indirect questions**
> I wonder / I was wondering ...
> Could you tell me ...
> Do you think ...
> I wanted to ask / I'd like to ask ...
> I'd like to know ...
> } *if* / question word + subject + verb
> Can you say ...

13 **Work in pairs. Make these questions less direct. Use the expressions from the Language Support box in Activity 12. The first one has been done for you.**

1 What tools did you use to collect statistical data?
I wanted to ask about the tools that you used to collect statistical data.
Can you say what tools you used to collect statistical data?
2 What is your attitude to the globalisation of education?
3 Where can we find your course online?
4 What challenges do educators face in your country?
5 Have you read about some similar research by Dr Jun Lui?
6 Can this approach be used in mixed-ability groups?
7 Have you got any experience in teaching a multinational group?

14 **Ask the questions that would lead to the answers below. Use the verb in brackets in your question.**

1 OK, here are the main points that I'll be covering. (*outline*)
2 Sure! A facilitator is someone who supports learning in different ways. (*define*)
3 Yes, a good example of facilitation is when a teacher probes and asks questions to get students to think more deeply. (*illustrate*)
4 Certainly. When I say 'flexibility', I mean that a facilitator should be ready to change their plan if it doesn't meet the needs of the group. (*clarify*)
5 Yes, I always stress the importance of equality in a discussion. The facilitator must identify signs of a developing hierarchy, should recognise all the members, but should not take sides in any developing debate. (*explain*)
6 Glad you asked that question! I believe facilitation is important in the classroom to create an environment of support, whether it's for a weekly one-hour group, or an intensive all-day process. (*justify*)

15 **Work in pairs. Prepare questions about the content of this lesson. Use the ideas in the list below. Then ask your teacher the questions.**

- the structure of a Q&A session
- the types and purposes of questions and comments from participants
- the structure of a good question
- the differences between direct and indirect questions

I wonder if it is possible to ask questions without the 'acknowledgement' element.

Follow-up

16 **Find (e.g. on YouTube) and listen to a presentation related to your specialism. Note down the ideas you would like to ask the presenter about. Make a list of clarifying and probing questions. Use this checklist to evaluate your questions:**

1 The questions are relevant to the talk.
2 All the elements of a good question are present.
3 The questions are polite.
4 The word order is correct.

Lesson 2 Responding to questions and comments

Lead-in

1 Read the words in the thought bubbles and decide what the topic of the presentation might be. What helped you decide?

globalise · international · identity · networking · profile · contact · linking · web · online · face-to-face

Listening

2 8 Listen to these sentences from a talk. Underline the words which are stressed by the speaker.

1 In the course of discussion one thing came out, which I thought we should put on the table immediately.
2 This was something that most people didn't do, which I know many of my colleagues do.
3 I've got a website, Twitter and Facebook presence.
4 And what we noticed is that most teachers don't have this.
5 And what we also realised is that because they don't have it, they are losing their international presence and in the globalised world you can't do that.

3 Read extracts 1–3 from three questions. Predict the key words that are missing.

1

> I was teaching the middle group of the class – the students that could keep up with what we were doing – while I had a group of [1] ____________ level students who were not [2] ____________ , and were [3] ____________ with the content, and [4] ____________ to move forward.

2

> You said that the [1] ____________ that your students write is assessed. Can you provide a bit of [2] ____________ about the way it's assessed? I'd be particularly interested to know what you use as the [3] ____________ for actually [4] ____________ the blog.

3

> In my classes I've had many difficulties with people texting their friends or even receiving [1] ____________ [2] ____________ during the lesson. How should I [3] ____________ that? I've tried [4] ____________ approaches but I still [5] ____________ this problem.

4 ⊙9 **Listen to the extracts and check your predictions.**

5 ⊙10 **Listen to a Q&A session and complete the second column of the table with *C* for a clarifying question or *P* for a probing one (see Activity 5 on page 24).**

Question	Type of question	Presenter's strategies
1		
2		
3		
4		
5		
6		

6 **Look at the list of strategies a presenter can use to answer questions. Which of these strategies do you use when you give a presentation?**

1 credit the person for asking the question
2 check that you understand the question
3 check that the questioner is satisfied with your answer
4 avoid giving an answer
5 admit that you cannot answer the question
6 refer the questioner to another source of information
7 reformulate the question in your own words
8 answer the question

7 ⊙10 **Listen to the Q&A session again and identify the strategies in Activity 6 that the presenter uses to answer the questions. Complete the table in Activity 5 with the appropriate numbers (1–8). More than one number can be used for each question.**

Language focus

8 **Match phrases a–g with strategies 1–8 in Activity 6. There is one strategy you do not need.**

a Sorry, that's not my field. But I'm sure Dr (*name*) could answer your question.
I'm afraid I don't know the answer to your question but I'll try to find out for you.
I'm afraid I'm not in a position to answer that. Perhaps (*name*) could help.
b OK, let me just repeat your question so everybody can hear it.
If I could just rephrase your question …
c Perhaps we could come back to that later.
I think the aim of this talk is to focus on … rather than …
I'd prefer to deal with that point later.
d If you want to find out more, look on this website: …
The journal (*name*) is a very useful source of information about that.
e Are you asking if …?
If I have understood you correctly, you mean … Is that right?
Sorry, is your question about …?
If I heard you correctly, you were asking …
f That was a great question.
I'm glad you asked that question.
Thanks for highlighting this. You raise an interesting issue.
g Does this answer your question? Is that OK?

9 ⊙ 10 Listen to the Q&A session again. Complete the sentences.

1 I was hoping someone would ____________ that ____________.
2 That's a __________________ question.
3 I'm not going to answer it in detail now because it's a ____________ question.
4 I hope that ____________ your ____________.
5 ____________ question!
6 Go to my ____________.
7 Sorry, I'm not ____________ whether I ____________ your question correctly.
8 Could you hear that question at the back? This lady is ____________ about our participants' ____________ and career promotion.
9 Sorry, but I'll have to ____________ back to that ____________, perhaps during the ____________ since we're __________________ of time.

10 Match each phrase in Activity 9 with a strategy in Activity 6.

Listening

11 ⊙ 11 Listen to five questions from different Q&A sessions and answer the questions below.

1 What was the topic of each presentation?
2 What does each questioner want to know?

12 ⊙ 11 Listen to the questions again, this time in the role of the presenter. Respond after the beep, using any strategy from Activity 8.

Follow-up

13 Prepare a short presentation about a topic you are interested in (e.g. your department, institution, research, a publication). Prepare no more than five slides for it. Use a tool such as PresentMe (https://present.me/content/) to record your presentation.

Organise a Q&A session. Use different strategies to deal with the questions from the audience.

Lesson 3 Paraphrasing and summarising

Lead-in

1 Work in pairs. Say how you would respond as a presenter in the situations below.

1 The room is rather noisy and you cannot hear somebody's question.
2 You are asked a very interesting question but the time for your presentation is over.
3 Your research does not deal with the question you have been asked.
4 A member of the audience asks you a very long and complicated question and you don't understand it.

Language focus

2 Read this indirect question. What strategy would you use to respond to it? Why?

> I wonder if 10 students in the experimental group and 10 students in the control group would be sufficient to conclusively determine the connections that you have identified.

3 Read sentences 1–3 and write down the techniques the presenters have used to paraphrase the question in Activity 2.

1 You mean you're not sure whether the number of students in the experimental and control groups is enough for us to make the connections we've made.
2 What you are asking is whether 20 participants is enough to confirm the reliability of the links we are trying to establish. Am I right?
3 In other words, you doubt the fact that as few as 10 in both experimental and control groups would be enough to explain the trends that we've stated.

4 Match the paraphrasing techniques in Activity 3 with examples a–c below. Sometimes more than one answer is possible.

a I believe that the idea of a classroom being a social space is very important. → In other words, you are trying to emphasise the importance of the idea of a classroom as a social space.

b It is necessary for our teachers to make their classrooms as little as possible like conventional classrooms. → So, your point is about the need to make modern classrooms different from traditional ones.

c The price of concentration on integrated studies, with the attendant neglect of a disciplinary base, will be the risk of disqualification from desirable postgraduate school and job opportunities. → Are you saying that students graduating from an interdisciplinary programme will be at a disadvantage when it comes to getting a job or a place on a postgraduate course?

5 **Work in pairs. Read statements 1–4 and follow the steps below to paraphrase them.**

1 In my opinion, the **term** 'group dynamics' **differs** significantly from the term 'rapport'. Rapport is more about creating a **positive atmosphere** while group dynamics are the **product** of the rapport that you build.
2 Sessions **begin** with creating a **group sense**, a feeling of working towards the **same goal**. This makes learners want to **continue** working.
3 What components should be **added** to **existing** teacher education **programmes** in order to ensure they handle **heterogeneous** classes more **effectively**?
4 Do you mean that this **approach** is more **appropriate** for **adolescents** or can it be also used with more **mature** learners?

- Choose words close in meaning to the words in bold.
- Decide what grammatical structure you can use to simplify each sentence.
- Paraphrase each sentence, using the expressions in the Language Support box.

Language Support: paraphrasing

What you're saying/asking is ...
So, if I understand your question, you want to know ... Am I right?
So, your point is about ...
Can I just check if I understood what you said? You mean ...
In other words, ...

Listening

6 12 **Listen to the presentation 'Changing paradigms' and complete the notes below. Write only key words.**

Reasons for changes

What causes problems?

Features of the old system

Presenter's suggestion

7 12 **Listen to the presentation again. Make notes of the points which you agree and disagree with.**

8 **Work in pairs. Make a list of clarifying and probing questions that you would like to ask the speaker. Present them to the whole group.**

9 **Read summaries A–C of the presentation in Activity 6. Choose the best one. Identify the features a good summary should have.**

A

The speaker mentioned two reasons for reforming public education. The first one is economic. It means that our task is to educate children to be able to live and work in the economies of the 21st century, but in his opinion, this is not easy.

The second reason is cultural, which means that educators want to pass on to children the cultural identity of their communities.

After that, the speaker presented his vision of the discrepancy between the existing system of education and what educators are trying to do now. In his opinion, the existing system was created for different purposes and for a different age, namely the age of the Industrial Revolution. The speaker gave some examples to prove that the organisation of schools is similar to that of factories. Due to this, children are taught in age groups and subjects are taught separately. The speaker used the analogy of a factory production line to characterise learning in schools.

In his view, drastic changes are required to meet the needs of modern learners and he calls it 'changing the paradigm'.

B

This was a very interesting presentation on how to reform public education. I quite agree with the reasons for reforming which the speaker mentioned, though I doubt that this can be explained by the fact that our system of education was designed for the time of the Industrial Revolution. On the whole, I believe it sounds quite reasonable that we should reconsider the system of education with a better understanding of modern learners' needs and learning styles.

C

The speaker started by mentioning economics and culture as the two main reasons for reforming public education. What he sees as the main reason for the problems in the existing education system is that it was designed for the age of the Industrial Revolution with the concepts of the Enlightenment in mind. The solution he offers is what he calls 'changing the paradigm', which means restructuring the system from one resembling a production line to one which caters for individual learners' needs.

Language focus

10 Read the summaries in Activity 9 again and complete the Language Support box with more phrases.

Language Support: summarising

At the beginning, ________________, Next, Further, ________________, Finally
The speaker pointed out / defined / assumed / ________________________

11 Prepare a short summary of the presentation in Activity 13 in Lesson 2 of this unit (see page 29). Read someone else's summary and use this checklist to evaluate it.

1 The summary is short.
2 It is logically structured.
3 The main idea of the talk is clear.
4 The speaker's words are properly paraphrased.

Follow-up

12 Find (e.g. on YouTube) a presentation on a topic of interest to you and listen to it. Note down the main ideas. Prepare a summary of the presentation and present it to the class. Use the checklist from Activity 11 to evaluate each other's summaries.

Unit 3 A round-table discussion

By the end of this unit you will be able to
- construct valid arguments
- evaluate and respond to arguments
- use appropriate language to manage a round-table discussion
- use appropriate language to participate in a round-table discussion

Lesson 1 Presenting arguments

Lead-in

1 Work in pairs. Discuss the questions.

1 Do you enjoy a good argument?
2 Why do you think people argue?
3 Which of the definitions below (a–b) gives the meaning of the word *argue* in academia and which gives its meaning in everyday life?
  a to give reasons to support or oppose an idea, opinion, etc.
  b to speak angrily to someone, telling them that you disagree with them

Reading

2 Read the text and complete notes 1–3.

An argument is an attempt to persuade someone by giving reasons. In critical thinking, an argument is a list of statements called reasons, supported by evidence and examples, and a conclusion. To provide an argument is to give reasons for accepting the conclusion. An argument usually begins with a statement of position, often called a thesis statement. Then the statement is backed up with reasons, evidence and examples. At the end, the position is restated or summed up in a conclusion.

Structure of an argument:
1 ______
2 a ______
  b ______
  c ______
3 ______

Listening

3 13 Listen to an argument and say how many reasons and pieces of evidence are given.

4 13 Listen again and complete the notes. Compare your notes with a partner.

Thesis statement: ______
Reason 1: ______
Evidence 1: ______
Reason 2: ______
Reason 3: ______
Conclusion: ______

5 ⊙ 14 **Listen to four arguments and add notes about the thesis statements and conclusions to the table. Write only key words.**

	Argument 1	Argument 2	Argument 3	Argument 4
Thesis statement	*Publications indispensable for academic career*			
Reasons			• • • *Have to give students tools for independent learning*	
Evidence and examples		*Only 4% finish course*		
Conclusion			*Have to be changes for us to be recognised worldwide*	

6 ⊙ 14 **Listen again and add notes about reasons, evidence and examples, if there are any, to the table in Activity 5.**

7 **Work in pairs. Compare your notes and complete the table in Activity 5 with any missing information.**

Language focus

8 ⊙ 15 **Listen to the extracts from the arguments in Activity 5 and complete them with words or phrases.**

1 The main ________ for this is that when you have publications, your rating becomes higher.
2 Another ________ is that the more you share your research with the public, the more …
3 I wholeheartedly ________ that the approach to university education in my country should be reconsidered …
4 ________ , the approach to education here is highly theoretical.
5 There is plenty of ________ in the literature for the idea that hands-on experience enhances learning.
6 So, ________ , there have to be changes in the system …

9 Add the highlighted phrases in Activity 8 to one of the Language Support boxes below.

Language Support: making a thesis statement

In my opinion, ...
I'm sure that ...
It is my belief that ...
It could be argued/asserted that ...
____

Language Support: providing evidence and examples

To support my point of view ...
To prove this statement ...
First of all ...
Not only ..., but also ...
Most recent research points to ...
Take for example (the case of) ...
______________________ ______________________
______________________ ______________________

Language Support: coming to conclusions

I should like to repeat once again that ...
To conclude, ...
Summing up, ...
On the whole, ...
Generally speaking, ...
____

10 Match expressions 1–6 with definitions a–f.

1 tricks of the trade
2 to be at the forefront
3 to spoon-feed someone
4 to climb the professional ladder
5 to be up to speed with something
6 to be on good terms with

a to have a positive relationship with
b methods that help to do a job better or faster
c to give someone so much help that they have no opportunity to think independently
d to have all the latest information about something
e to move to a higher position at work
f to be in the most noticeable or important position

11 **Substitute the underlined phrases with appropriate phrases from the box. Change the form where necessary.**

to gain someone's respect	to miss a deadline	to build rapport	
to facilitate learning	subject matter	scientific discovery	to enrol for a course

1 It takes time <u>to develop good relationships</u> with students.
2 If you want <u>to be a member of the course</u>, contact the staff.
3 You will drop out if you <u>do not complete the tasks on time</u>.
4 In a university course, not only <u>the contents of a subject</u>, but also academic skills are taught.
5 This sequence of activities is aimed at <u>making learning easier</u>.
6 Effort is needed to <u>win the esteem</u> of students.
7 Nowadays, <u>finding new information in science</u> is a group achievement, not an individual one.

12 **Work in pairs. Use your own ideas to complete the sentences.**

1 To be on good terms with my students and build rapport, I ...
2 To be at the forefront of their field a university teacher has to ...
3 It's not a good idea to spoon-feed students, because ...
4 I keep up to speed with ... by ...
5 To climb the professional ladder, it is important for a researcher to ...
6 If students who enrol for my course miss deadlines, I ...
7 To facilitate learning, I use the following methods: firstly, ... , secondly, ...

Speaking

13 **Plan your argument for one of the statements below. Write an outline as in Activity 4. Note down the language you need to complete the task.**

1 Being aware of copyright laws is / is not important for academics.
2 Higher education should / should not collaborate with business and industry and develop life skills.
3 Being a university teacher means / doesn't mean having knowledge of only one area of study.
4 The use of technology affects / does not affect the quality of learning and teaching.

14 **Work in pairs. Present your argument to your partner. Use the language from the Language Support boxes in Activity 9.**

15 **Agree or disagree with the ideas given by your partner, using the language from this lesson.**

Follow-up

16 **Work in pairs. Reword the thesis statements below to turn them into conclusions. Use phrases from the Language Support box 'coming to conclusions' on page 35.**

1 It is my belief that any university teacher has to be a researcher.
2 Students ought to be given more choice and autonomy.
3 The teacher–student ratio is one of the factors that determine the quality of a university.

17 **Work in pairs. Think of reasons, evidence and examples to support one of the statements in Activity 16. Note them down.**

Lesson 2 Evaluating arguments

Lead-in

1 Read the quotations below. Do you agree with them? Why? / Why not? Which meaning of *argument* (everyday or academic) is used in each of them?

That's the beauty of argument: if you argue correctly, you're never wrong. (Christopher Buckley)
Argument cannot be answered with insults. Kindness is strength; anger blows out the lamp of the mind. (Robert G. Ingersoll)
What's all this love of arguing? No one ever convinces anyone else. (Leo Tolstoy)

Language focus

Tip:
'Logical relations' are relations between ideas that make a text connected.

2 Match logical relations 1–5 with extracts A–E.

1 cause and effect
2 comparison and contrast
3 addition and reinforcement
4 exemplification and evidence
5 time

A
The research has been criticised for several reasons. It used a sample that was not representative enough and the results were controversial. Moreover, the statistical analysis was found to be faulty.

B
Writing for academic publication requires effort and concentration. Consequently, if you concentrate on your paper every day, even for short periods, , your progress will be noticeable.

C
Initially, you will submit your paper and wait for a review. As soon as you get it, start correcting your paper, following the reviewer's suggestions.

D
The first step will be studying the recent publications in your field. It is important, in particular, to understand the content, focus, structure and style.

E
A panel discussion, like a round-table discussion, brings a number of people together to discuss a preassigned question. Unlike round-tables, panels have an audience who may also ask and discuss questions.

3 Add the highlighted words in Activity 2 to the appropriate Language Support box below.

Language Support: cause and effect

Cause		Effect
as because (of) therefore	since due to (the fact that)	as a result as a result of thus so

Language Support: addition and reinforcement

additionally	besides	as well as
specifically	what is more	
especially	indeed	

Language Support: comparison and contrast

Comparison	Contrast
in the same way likewise similarly	by/in contrast conversely on the contrary

4 Use a linking word or phrase from the Language Support boxes to connect the sentences in 1–4 logically.

1. In a round-table discussion participants do not make presentations or distribute handouts. They are allowed to express their opinions for two or three minutes.
2. A paper is an oral presentation, supported by visual aids, by a speaker or a group of speakers . In a poster presentation the main emphasis is on the visuals.
3. Conference preparation takes a lot of time and effort. It requires someone with excellent organisational skills.
4. In the Conclusions section of an article you summarise the ideas and draw conclusions. At the end of a presentation it is necessary to cover the main points and make a summary.

5 Work in pairs. Complete the sentences in a logical way.

1. Since it is important for a teacher to build rapport with his or her students, ...
2. Rapid communications should not exceed 5,000 words. By contrast, ...
3. Distance-learning courses demand effort and commitment. As a result, ...
4. An abstract of an article outlines the methods and the outcomes of research. Likewise, a conclusion ...
5. Interdisciplinary education has to deal with a number of problems, specifically, ...

6 Write pairs of logically connected sentences, using prompts as in the example.

subject matter / research activities
Those students who are involved in scientific research demonstrate a deeper understanding of the subject matter. In contrast, those not participating in research activities may have difficulty realising how theory is put into practice.

1 build rapport / gain respect

____

____

2 publish or perish / climb a professional ladder

____

____

3 enrol for a course / scientific discovery

____

____

7 Work in pairs. Listen to your partner's sentences and say which logical relation he/she has expressed.

Reading

8 Rewrite these false statements to make a checklist for a good argument.

1 Some elements of the structure of an argument are omitted.

____

2 All the parts of the argument are disconnected.

____

3 There are some contradictory points.

____

4 The evidence which is given is unreliable and irrelevant.

____

5 The tone is emotional.

____

9 Work in pairs. Read the arguments and evaluate them according to the criteria in Activity 8. (See Activity 2 on page 33 for the structure of an argument.)

A

Modern technologies certainly bring in lots of opportunities into our lives, but it cannot be denied that they have drawbacks as well as advantages. The first point to make is that technologies not only support but also inhibit learning. Let me illustrate this point with an example. Teachers, including those in my department, complain about the abuse of mobile devices in university classrooms and debate how to make students more focussed in class. Many students can't even concentrate outside class. But they successfully complete the work on my course using our university's learning management system.

This argument does not have a conclusion.
The parts are disconnected: the speaker starts discussing the drawbacks of technologies in learning, but then talks about students' concentration outside class.
There are some contradictory points: the speaker argues that students cannot concentrate because of technology, but then says that they successfully complete their work online.

B

> The quality of research results in our field is not as high as it used to be, say, 30 years ago, and I'll explain why. There is pressure to be published. The time one can allow to prepare and carry out research, analyse the results and prepare a publication is quite short. Racing to meet deadlines, we omit important details. Modern technology helps to process data quickly. We have much larger bodies of data today. There is no time to be thorough and meticulous. The research is of lower quality.

C

> From my point of view, plagiarism is one of the burning issues of today. Today, when technology has given us access to seemingly unlimited sources of data, plagiarism has become the norm. I hate to say it, but everyone plagiarises. Most of all, students. It seems 'copy-and-paste' is their favourite function. According to research, 70% of students' work contains plagiarism. Not only that, but academics do the same. A recent inspection in one of the universities revealed that History theses were more than 50% plagiarised! This shows no respect for copyright and the intellectual effort of others!

Speaking

10 Read the Language Support box and write *A* next to the phrases that express agreement and *D* next to those expressing disagreement.

Language Support: responding to arguments

1 That's exactly what I think.
2 I might agree with the point about ... , but ...
3 That's a good point.
4 I'm afraid I have to disagree on the point about ... and I feel compelled to say that ...
5 I totally agree.
6 I find it interesting that ... , but on the other hand ...

11 Work in pairs. Decide how the arguments in Activity 9 can be improved. Consider both the language and the logical structure of each argument.

12 Work in groups. Report the improved arguments to another pair.

13 Evaluate your classmates' arguments according to the criteria in Activity 8. Respond to their arguments using the language from the Language Support box above.

Follow-up

14 Outline an argument on one of the topics below.

- Participating in international conferences: is it worth the effort?
- Can all university teachers be at the forefront of their areas of interest?
- Teaching other subjects in English: a waste of time or an opportunity?

15 Work in pairs. Present your argument to a partner.

16 Respond to your partner's argument using the expressions from the Language Support box.

Lesson 3 Discussion matters

Lead-in

1 Have you ever participated in a round-table discussion? What was discussed? What roles did the participants have?

Language focus

2 Work in pairs. Choose the word in italics in each sentence that best suits an academic context.

1 The 'publish-or-perish' imperative shifts the *intensity / emphasis / strength* away from real teaching.
2 The 'publish-or-perish' system causes a lot of stress, not only to young academics, but also to more *established / advanced / settled* scholars.
3 Citations are intended to provide *indication / information / evidence* that publications are actually read.
4 Writing scholarly publications is a(n) *insistent / crucial / urgent* aspect of academic work.
5 Be ready to react as quickly as possible when required to make *modifications / repairs / amendments* to your publication.
6 This is a way to *maintain / retain / ascertain* communication with other researchers.

3 Paraphrase the underlined phrases, using language from Activity 2.

1 Are <u>experienced academics</u> under pressure to get published?
____
2 Can you <u>give any supporting facts</u> for the argument that publications are <u>a highly important feature</u> of academic work? ______________
3 What aspects of academic work <u>move the focus</u> from actual teaching?
____
4 Do you usually have to <u>make changes</u> to your publications after reviewing?
____
5 How do you <u>keep in contact</u> with colleagues abroad? ______________

4 Work in pairs. Answer the paraphrased questions in Activity 3.

Reading

5 Identify the elements of the following arguments (see Activity 2 on page 33) and put them in the correct order.

Argument 1

a First of all, publishing is a way to maintain communication with other researchers. Research is not an individual effort today, as many institutions around the world are working on the same problem and have to share their knowledge to get important results.
b Secondly, universities demand publications from their employees. If you don't publish, you won't get a position.
c Writing scholarly publications is a crucial aspect of academic work.
d In short, publishing is crucial for research, your career and your own satisfaction.
e But that's not all. Academics are driven by intrinsic motives. They get satisfaction from writing for publication. (You know, it really happens!)

Argument 2

a Therefore, impact factors* are not reliable and can be manipulated.
b Finally, articles can be cited because they demonstrate research of low quality.
c Citation also has its issues.
d Some articles are cited without being read. They are so-called secondary citations.
e Citations provide evidence that publications are actually read. However, citations can include self-citations, that is reference to oneself, which can boost the citation rate.

*impact factor: a measure that shows the average number of citations of an article in an academic journal within a period of time

6 **The sentences in Activities 2 and 3 are from a discussion. What was the topic of the discussion? What matters were being discussed?**

Listening

7 16 **Listen to a round-table discussion and say if each statement is true or false.**

1 The moderator introduces the participants.
2 Dan does not agree with Ann about the importance of publications.
3 The moderator interrupts Dan because his answer is irrelevant.
4 Paul wants to be the first to answer the second question.
5 Dan agrees with Paul about the features of a good publication.
6 Dan and Ann have different views about the pressure to publish.
7 The moderator finishes the discussion by saying that academics should not publish.

8 **Work in pairs. Put the words in the correct order to make expressions.**

1 this? / your / on / What's / view ____________
2 couldn't / more. / I / agree ____________
3 but/ 're going to / to interrupt you, / we / that issue / later. / discuss / Sorry

____
4 on / I / first / this? / come in / Can ____________
5 I / exactly / see / That's / it. / how ____________
6 the /back / to / of ... / Coming / issue ____________
7 with/ afraid/ I have/ Dan./ I'm/ to agree ____________

9 16 **Listen to the discussion again and check your answers in Activity 8.**

10 **Match headings a–c with Language Support boxes 1–3.**

a taking the initiative
b shifting the topic
c iinterrupting politely

Language Support: 1 ____________

What you are saying is very interesting, but let's focus on the original topic.
I'd just like to say that ...
If I could just interrupt for a moment ...

____

Language Support: 2 ______________________

I'd like to be the first to answer.
May I give you my opinion?
Can I chip in with an idea?
If I could just come in here.
____

Language Support: 3 ______________________

Now let's turn to ...
Moving on, let us discuss the issue of ...
Let's focus on another aspect of ...
____

11 **Add some of the expressions from Activity 8 to the appropriate Language Support box in Activity 10.**

Speaking

12 **Work in groups. Have a round-table discussion. Follow the steps below.**

1 Choose a topic for the round-table discussion. For example:
- participation in conferences
- preparing publications
- teaching other subjects in English.

2 Formulate the questions to discuss within the topic.
3 Choose the moderator.
4 Allow 7–10 minutes for:
- the participants to outline their answers to the questions
- the moderator to study the guidelines below and plan the discussion.

5 Have a round-table discussion. Use the expressions from the Language Support boxes.

Guidelines for the moderator

1 Welcome and introduce the participants.
2 Let everyone speak.
3 Interrupt politely if one of the participants speaks for a long time or does not stick to the topic.
4 Paraphrase or ask clarification questions if necessary.
5 Do not give evaluative judgements.
6 Do not answer your own questions.
7 Thank the participants for their contributions.
8 Summarise the discussion.

Follow-up

13 **Evaluate your participation in the round-table discussion, using the checklist below.**

	Never	From time to time	All the time
I contributed to the discussion.			
I was polite and did not interrupt unless a speaker had finished.			
I did not speak for long and I let others express their views. I reacted to what others said but was not defensive.			

Overall, I am *satisfied / dissatisfied* with my performance.

Next time I will *(choose the appropriate options)*

- provide more arguments and support them more strongly
- be more polite
- speak for a shorter time and listen to the opinions of others
- use more appropriate language for different functions
- do the same as I did in this session.

Unit 4 A panel discussion

By the end of this unit you will be able to
- prepare for, and take part in, a panel discussion as a moderator and panellist
- summarise what different people say in a panel discussion

Lesson 1 Preparing for a panel discussion

Lead-in

1 Work in pairs. Answer the questions and then discuss them as a whole class.

1 What is a panel discussion?
2 Have you ever taken part in a panel discussion? If yes, in what capacity?
3 Whose role, do you think, is more difficult: that of a panellist or a moderator? Why?

Listening

2 17 Listen to an extract from a podcast about moderators of panel discusssions and choose the statement that sums it up best. Give reasons for your choice.

a A panel moderator has a lot of responsibilities during the discussion.
b A good panel moderator is crucial to the success of a panel discussion.
c A panel moderator's job is to control everything during the discussion.

3 17 Listen again and fill in the gaps.

A moderator is expected to

1 set the __________ for both the panellists and the audience.
2 provide the __________ and coherence in the panel.
3 ensure __________ participation from the panellists.
4 make sure that the __________ in the audience have an opportunity to ask questions and get answers.
5 control the flow of the discussion, summarise the main ideas and link them together, so that the discussion has a sense of __________ and complete __________ of the topic.
6 __________ the time.

4 Match skills 1–6 in Activity 3 with functions a–h below. More than one function can be matched with each skill.

Skill 1 __________ Skill 4 __________
Skill 2 __________ Skill 5 __________
Skill 3 __________ Skill 6 __________

a opening an event
b explaining the focus of the discussion
c summing up a talk/discussion
d paraphrasing a question/statement
e interrupting politely
f directing the discussion
g keeping the discussion on track
h closing the event

5 ⊙ 18 **Listen to a second extract from the podcast and choose the correct option.**

The speaker talks about what she does to ensure success

a before the panel discussion
b during the panel discussion
c after the panel discussion
d in the course of the entire event.

6 ⊙ 18 **Listen again and complete the flow chart, showing the sequence of steps the speaker recommends.**

1 ______________________________

2 ______________________________

3 ______________________________

4 ______________________________

7 ⊙ 18 **Complete the questions the speaker asks her colleagues in order to prepare questions for the panel. Then listen and check your answers.**

1 Suppose you attended my panel, what points ______________________________?
2 What do you think you might ______________________________?
3 What do you think you'd like ______________________________?
4 Here are some questions ____________ our audience attendees would like to be addressed.
5 Is there something ____________ to add?

Language focus

8 **Compare these questions with those in Activity 7. What is the difference in the wording? What is the effect of this difference?**

1 What points do you want to make?
2 What do you want to hear about from the experts?
3 What do you want to learn from them?
4 Here are some questions our audience attendees would like to be addressed.
5 Is there something you want to add?

9 **Make these questions more tentative/hypothetical. Change the form of some words as necessary.**

1 What do I need to do to ensure the success of my panel?
2 How does the topic of the panel fit into the conference theme?
3 What do you want to learn from the experts?
4 What sort of expertise can you offer?
5 How much time do you need to cover your point?

10 Write definitions of the phrases below.

1 to offer expertise ______
2 to make a point ______
3 to address questions ______
4 to put together a list ______
5 to get in touch with someone ______
6 to cover all the key points ______
7 to assume something ______
8 to let someone know ______
9 a series of questions ______
10 to make sure ______

11 Use the phrases in Activity 11 to paraphrase the sentences below. Make other changes as necessary.

Panellists are usually people who can [1]give expert opinions on the issues under discussion. It's important that you help them [2]to communicate with each other some time before the conference. Otherwise they might fail [3]to deal with all the main issues that you have on your list. It isn't wise [4]to think that even experienced panellists will be able to stick to the point while talking.

My advice is: identify potential attendees among your colleagues and ask them what [5]ideas they would like to talk about. This helps to decide what questions a panellist should [6]deal with. It takes time [7]to compile a list of questions for a discussion. When you have one, you are halfway to success.

Always [8]inform everyone in the panel about how it will go. And remember [9]to check that you know how the names of the panellists are pronounced. It is quite an issue in events with international participation.

Speaking

12 Start preparing for your panel. Follow the steps below.

1 Choose one of the subthemes that are on the diagram of your conference (see Activity 5 on page 15).
2 Go around your class and ask your classmates as potential attendees what questions they would like the experts in your panel to address. Ask tentative/hypothetical questions.

Follow-up

13 Prepare for your panel. Follow the steps below.

1 Research online the topic/subtheme you have chosen for your panel. See how it fits into the theme of the conference.
2 Identify three or four people in your class who might be useful on your panel as experts. Contact your panellists via email: explain the purpose of your writing and how the panel will work. With their help, put together a list of questions and a panel handout. (See Activity 7.)
3 Keep your list of questions and handout for Lesson 3.

Lesson 2 Summarising a discussion

Lead-in

1 Work in pairs. Discuss the questions and then share your thoughts with the whole class.

How is summarising from one source different from summarising from many sources?
How is summarising a written text different from summarising a spoken source?

Language focus

2 Add prefixes to words 1–6 so that they have the opposite meaning.

1 clear __________
2 acceptable __________
3 relevant __________
4 capable __________
5 resolvable __________
6 definite __________

3 Paraphrase sentences 1–5 using language from Activity 2.

1 It seems this problem cannot be solved.
____
2 You have mentioned an issue that is not related to the topic.
____
3 This objective is difficult to understand.
____
4 And what about the students who don't have the ability to complete the task?
____
5 We cannot accept such behaviour.
____

4 Match the underlined expressions in the text with their equivalents a–g .

Though interdisciplinary education has [1]<u>diverse benefits</u>, I'd like to offer some [2]<u>decisive arguments against it</u>. Firstly, students are [3]<u>deprived of the opportunity</u> to study the [4]<u>core subjects</u> in depth. Secondly, students can't [5]<u>sustain focus</u> and they lose concentration. Lastly, there is [6]<u>a certain reluctance</u> among employers to hire graduates with double diplomas. To conclude, the problem of interdisciplinary education [7]<u>deserves close attention</u>, as there are some important issues that have to be considered.

a main disciplines
b a kind of unwillingness
c not given the chance
d is worthy of careful consideration
e keep their concentration
f various advantages
g clear counter-arguments

Listening

5 Work in pairs. Discuss the questions.

1 What are interdisciplinary studies?
2 What are the benefits of interdisciplinary studies, if any?
3 What is the general attitude to interdisciplinary studies in your institution?

6 **Read the steps for a 'welcome to a panel discussion'. What order would you put them in?**

a Introduction of the panellists.
b Explanation of the procedures and rules.
c Introduction of the first question to discuss.
d Greeting.
e Introduction of the topic.

7 **19 Listen to a moderator welcoming everybody to a panel discussion about interdisciplinary studies. In what order does she do the steps in Activity 6?**

8 **Work in pairs. Discuss what kind of language helps you identify that a problem is being discussed.**

9 **20 Listen to the first part of the panel discussion introduced in Activity 7. Read the description of it below and fill in the gaps with an appropriate word or a short phrase. Compare answers with a partner.**

Derek took the initiative and offered to speak first. He expressed the opinion that interdisciplinary studies cause [1] ______________ .

He listed the following issues:

- there are no clear [2] ______________
- what is meant by 'connections between disciplines' is [3] ______________
- no one says what the results [4] ______________ .

Ellie agreed, saying that [5] ______________ are seen as unimportant and irrelevant. She also said that on these programmes it is impossible to [6] ______________ the result.

Other speakers mentioned other problems, such as:

- high [7] ______________
- teachers have to be borrowed from the [8] ______________ .

10 **Work in pairs. Make a list of the problems that interdisciplinary studies can cause.**

11 **20 Listen again and write down the expressions the speakers use for functions 1–3.**

1 to take the initiative and offer to answer
  a *Let me be the first to answer.*
  b ______________
2 to check understanding
  a *Am I right in assuming that ...?*
  b ______________
3 to refer to knowledge – your own or someone else's
  a *I'm very aware of what Derek is saying.*
  b ______________

Speaking and Listening

12 Work in pairs. Make a list of phrases that can be used in a summary to do the following:

1 to describe what the speakers said
The first speaker stated that ...
He added/went on to say that ...

2 to compare the speakers' opinions
The speakers agreed about/on/that ...
Nevertheless, they expressed different opinions about ...

3 to draw a conclusion
Overall it can be concluded that ...
To summarise, ...

13 Work in pairs. Orally summarise the discussion in Activity 9. Use your notes and the language from Activity 12. Follow the steps below.

1 Introduce the topic.
2 Outline the main ideas the speakers expressed.
3 Say what the speakers agreed or disagreed about.
4 Draw a conclusion.

14 ⊙21 Listen to the second part of the discussion and complete the notes below. Write only key words.

1 Examples of successful interdisciplinary communication:
 a *the use of X-rays in genetics* ________
 b ________
2 Breakthroughs usually happen at ________
3 Interdisciplinary education develops the ability:
 a ________
 b ________
4 The moderator concludes by saying that interdisciplinary study is ________ but there are ________ about its use in undergraduate training.

Follow-up

15 Work in pairs. Orally summarise the whole discussion. Use the checklist below to evaluate your partner's performance.

1 The speaker followed the steps in Activity 13.
2 The speaker used the language from the unit.
3 The speaker did not express his or her opinion on the topic.
4 The speaker included all the necessary information from the discussion.

16 Find a discussion on the internet that is of interest to you. In class, summarise it to a partner.

Lesson 3 Closing effectively

Lead-in

1 Look through the list of common difficulties that may occur during question time in a panel discussion. Think of ways of handling them.

1 The questioner is not sure whether he/she can ask his/her question.
2 The questioner speaks in a low voice.
3 The questioner is sitting at the front and the people at the back can't hear him/her.
4 The questioner asks more than one question.
5 The question is complicated.
6 The answer is too long.
7 There are no questions.

Reading

2 Read the text and find some solutions to the problems listed in Activity 1.

It is very important that the audience know how questions will be handled by the facilitator. It is common practice that attendees simply raise their hands to let the moderator know that they have a question. To show a member of the audience that you are ready to take their question, make eye contact with them. After they have given their question, repeat it to make sure that everyone is following.

Sometimes people ask more than one question. Then you have to decide whether to take all of them or choose one. What you decide will depend largely on the time available. Look at your panel and ask who would like to take the question first.

Sometimes a question is not well structured. Then you need to paraphrase it. Offer your own understanding but ask the questioner to confirm that your paraphrase is right.

If an answer is long, it is useful to summarise it before taking another question.

Be prepared with some questions of your own in case the audience remains silent.

Speaking

3 Read the sentences below and identify the situation the moderator is dealing with.

[1]You're making some great points, John, [2]but we're pressed for time. [3]We'll come back to you if time permits.

4 Match functions a–c with the parts of the speech 1–3 in Activity 3.

a mentioning shortage of time
b suggesting another time/place
c showing appreciation

5 **In extracts 1–3 identify functions a–c in Activity 4.**

1

Thanks for those great ideas, John, but we need to watch the time. So, I'm going to ask Justin to give his point of view and then maybe you can meet some of the audience after the discussion to talk about this more.

2

That's such a great idea, it would be an interesting topic for a full panel discussion, but let's focus again on …

3

You offer an interesting new perspective, John. I'd like to look at it in more detail, but unfortunately our time is really limited. Let's hear what Justin has to say.

6 **Work in groups of four. Take turns to role play ways of interrupting a speaker.**

7 **Look through the 'To do' list below and tick the things you need to do to close a discussion effectively. Give reasons for your choices.**

1 summarise the main conclusions from the discussion
2 thank all the panellists for their expertise
3 hand out the evaluation sheets
4 thank the attendees for coming
5 direct the attendees to where the next sessions are
6 make some notes on what went well and what needed improvement
7 write a thank-you note to each panellist

8 22 **Listen to the moderator and tick the things in Activity 7 that she does .**

9 **Role play a panel discussion. Use the questions you prepared in Activity 13 in Lesson 1 of this unit (see page 47).**

Moderator: With your teacher, prepare the room for your panel. If necessary, hold a pre-panel meeting with the panellists.

Panellists: Review the questions for the panel and how you are going to respond.

Attendees: Study the panel handout and think of two to three questions. You might need to change or modify them depending on how the discussion goes.

Follow-up

10 Use this form to assess your performance as moderator.

Self-Evaluation Card for Moderator

	Yes/No
1 Organisation:	
– Was the room prepared well?	
2 Opening:	
– Did I say everything I needed to say?	
3 Handling the panel:	
– Did I manage the time effectively?	
– Did I summarise effectively?	
– Did I make sure that all the panellists participated equally?	
4 Question-taking:	
– Did I keep control effectively?	
– Did I ensure a smooth flow of questions and answers?	
5 Closing:	
– Did I say everything that was necessary?	

Module wrapping-up

1 You have finished Module 1. Congratulations! Reflect on the module and evaluate your progress. Read the statements in the table below and tick them if you agree with them.

Module 1	
I can create a timeline for a major academic event in English.	
I can write a call for papers in English.	
I can ask questions in English in a Q&A session.	
I can respond to questions in English in a Q&A session.	
I can paraphrase what I hear in English orally.	
I can summarise other speakers' ideas orally.	
I can construct a valid argument in English.	
I can respond to an argument in English.	
I can manage a round-table discussion in English.	
I can manage a panel discussion.	

2 What do you need to improve further? Set yourself some goals for further development. Use the SMART principle: goals should be Specific, Measurable, Achievable, Realistic, Time-bound.

3 Share your responses to the module with the whole class.

Module 2

Writing for publication

In this module you will:

- write an article about your research
- select a journal for your article
- write a covering letter to the journal editor

Unit 1 Preparing to write

By the end of this unit you will be able to
- identify key information in guidelines for contributors to international journals
- compare and contrast information from guidelines for authors
- recognise the types and structure of academic articles
- choose a journal in which to publish an article
- prepare a title and abstract for an academic article in your own subject area

Lesson 1 Guidelines for authors

Lead-in

1 Read the statement below and fill in the gaps with the percentages that you think are possible. Say which group of researchers you belong to and explain why.

[1]______________ per cent of researchers prefer first to write an article and then edit it according to the guidelines for authors. However, [2]______________ per cent prefer to read the authors' guidelines first and then follow them when they write their manuscript for submission.

2 Read the quotation below. Do you agree with it? Why? / Why not? What might be in these instructions, do you think?

Careful preparation before starting to write will save you time and spare you frustration later on. In publishing, as in everything else in life, it pays TO READ THE INSTRUCTIONS. (Ann M. Körner)

Reading

2 Read Texts 1 and 2 quickly and tick the boxes in the table if they contain the information in 1–5. Ignore any words you don't know.

	Text 1	Text 2
1 Age of the journal		
2 Scope (the range of subjects covered by the journal)		
3 Audience		
4 Recommendations about the language		
5 Time from submission to publication		

Text 1

Network Science is a new journal for a new discipline – one using the network paradigm to inform research, methodology, and applications from many fields across the natural, social, engineering and informational sciences. The journal welcomes contributions from researchers in all relevant areas working on network theory, methods, and data.

Manuscript Preparation

Network Science is intended for a broad, interdisciplinary audience. Please avoid jargon and give adequate explanations of concepts and methods that may be unfamiliar to academic readers from different fields. However, please assume that our readers are familiar with introductory ideas in network science. It is not necessary in submissions to define terms such as *centrality*, *density* or *degree distribution*.

Length:

As an interdisciplinary journal, *Network Science* encourages articles from different fields that often have different publishing standards. In general, the length of an article should be between 20 and 40 pages, including footnotes and references, but the editors are open to exceptions if needed. We are not currently accepting book or software reviews.

Abstracts:

Abstracts should be no more than 200 words and should include the main aims of the paper, the methods and specific data source if applicable, and the conclusions. Please include up to 10 keywords that should accompany the article.

Text 2

Geological Magazine, established in 1864, is one of the oldest and best-known periodicals in the Earth Sciences. It publishes original papers, book reviews and rapid communications about all aspects of the geosciences. *Geological Magazine* has a particular strength in providing a niche for interdisciplinary papers on regional geology and Earth history that would be of interest to geologists from many different specialisms. Papers of any length are considered, provided that the length is justifiable.

The Editors welcome original, creative, high-quality contributions suitable for the journal's international readership. There are no page charges for papers published in *Geological Magazine*, though there is a charge for printing of colour images. Online reproduction of colour images is free of charge.

Original Articles

This category is intended for full-scale research studies that fit within the journal's scope. There is no page limit; however, papers should be as concise as clarity permits. They should include a summary of up to 250 words, accompanied by 4–7 keywords.

Rapid Communications
This category is designed for concisely written research reports for which rapid publication is considered desirable. Papers in this category should not exceed six printed pages of the journal (approximately 5,000-word equivalents), including an abstract of no more than 100 words, and 4–7 keywords. *Rapid Communications* will normally be published within six months of submission. To meet this schedule, authors will be required to make revisions with minimal delay.

Book Reviews
Book Reviews are published on selected books that fall within the journal's scope, on topics that the Book Review Editor considers to be of general interest to readers of *Geological Magazine*. *Book Reviews* are published by the invitation of the Book Review Editor and should not be submitted independently.

3 Read Texts 1 and 2 again. Focus on the main instructions for authors and complete the table.

Instructions	*Network Science*	*Geological Magazine*
1 Types of articles	• *Articles from different fields* • *No book reviews* • ______________	
2 Article length		• *Original papers: no page limit* • *Rapid communications:* ______________
3 Abstract length		
4 Manuscript preparation		*Not mentioned*
5 Submission procedure	*Not mentioned*	
6 Charges		

4 Work in pairs. What might be missing from Texts 1 and 2? Make a list of any additional information that authors may need in order to get their papers published in a journal.

Language focus

5 From Texts 1 and 2, make a list of words describing different elements of an academic article, e.g. *footnotes.*

6 Work in pairs. Say which of the elements from Activity 5 you always, often or never include in your articles. Give your reasons.

7 Match the words and phrases (1–11) with the ones that are similar in meaning (a–m). More than one match may be possible.

1	readers	a	suitable for
2	journal	b	summary
3	submissions	c	area
4	intended for	d	readership
5	contain	e	periodical
6	field	f	paper
7	abstract	g	audience
8	article	h	designed for
9	studies	i	include
10	fit within	j	contributions
11	applicable for/to	k	fall within
		l	specialism
		m	research

8 Complete Text 3 with words from the box.

contains contributions editor intended to journal paper readership research suited

Text 3

Teaching Physics is a long-established [1]__________, included in the Science Citation Index Expanded. It is a biannual, peer-reviewed periodical [2]__________ provide an overview of [3]__________ in physics education to its international [4]__________ of researchers and practitioners. Each issue [5]__________ articles on various aspects of teaching physics in universities.

We invite [6]__________ to any section in the journal. In the first instance, contributors are advised to contact the [7]__________ to discuss their proposed [8]__________ and the section for which it is best [9]__________.

Speaking

9 Work in pairs. Compare the information in Texts 1, 2 and 3. What new pieces of information for authors are mentioned in Text 3?

10 Work in groups. Find the similarities between *Network Science* (NS), *Geological Magazine* (GM) and *Teaching Physics* (TP). Report them to the class. Use the table in Activity 3 and expressions in the Language Support box below.

> **Language Support: comparison – similarity**
>
> Both NS and GM publish ...
> TP and GM are similar regarding / with respect to / in terms of ...
> NS, as well as GM, asks/requires ...
> Like NS, GM accepts ...

11 Work in groups and note down the differences between *Network Science*, *Geological Magazine* and *Teaching Physics*. Compare your group findings with the whole class. Use the Language Support box below.

> **Language Support: comparison – contrast**
>
> NS is (*newer*) than GM, while/but GM is (*much better known*).
> TP has a narrower focus than ...
> Unlike NS, GM (publishes) ...
> In comparison with TP, NS is very (*new*).
> In contrast to NS, TP focuses on ...
> The guidelines for GM contain advice about ... By contrast, nothing is said about it in (*NS*).
> TP is (*more relevant to*) ... , whereas NS is aimed at ...
> Although GM is (*more prominent*), NS ...

Listening

12 Work in pairs. Discuss which of the factors below may influence your choice of journal in which to publish your paper. Compare your views with another pair.

1 The scope and aims of the journal are relevant to your paper.
2 The journal provides open access to some articles.
3 The journal impact factor is reasonably high.
4 The page charges are low.
5 The time taken to accept or reject a paper is quite short.

13 23 Listen to a professor giving advice on how to choose a journal. Tick the factors in Activity 12 that he mentions.

14 23 Listen to the professor again and answer the questions below.

1 How many parts are there in his talk? What does each of them focus on?
2 How many points does he make in the last part of his talk?
3 How were you able to identify the number of points?

Follow-up

15 Look on the internet for journals in your own subject area and read their guidelines for authors. Report orally on what the guidelines require. Which journal would you like your article to be published in? Why?

Lesson 2 Article structure

Lead-in

1 Work in two teams. Each team should find the best visual way to present the conventional structure of a research article.

2 Compare your visuals. Do they have the same sections?

Listening

3 24 Listen to a librarian talking about different academic publications and complete the first column of the table.

Types of article	Key words and phrases
1	
2	
3	
4	

4 24 Listen again. Complete the second column with the key words and phrases which help to identify each type of article.

5 Work in pairs. Discuss which types of articles you have submitted or are going to submit.

Reading

6 Read Text 1 (on page 62) and choose the most appropriate title for it from titles 1–4. Say what type of text it is.

1 The importance of newspapers in studying people's mental health
2 Recurring themes in newspaper reports on depression
3 Media representation of depression in young people
4 Newspaper coverage helps recognise symptoms of depression

Text 1

A__________ [1]Newspaper media are an important source of information regarding mental health and have a significant influence on people's awareness of mental health issues. [2]Depression in young people has seen increasing media attention in recent years, but few studies have examined media representation of mental health, specifically in young people. [3]The current study used a quantitative approach to examine the words used in reports concerning depression in young people, in Irish broadsheets, published between 2007 and 2011. [4]The aims of the study were to identify recurring themes in Irish newspaper reports on depression in young people, and to examine the textual patterns that are repeated in reporting these themes.

B__________ [5]A sample of 269 texts, containing 176 223 words, was collected from three Irish broadsheet newspapers, using the search terms 'depression' or 'depressed' or 'mental health' and 'youth' or 'young people'. [6]A corpus-based approach was used to examine word frequencies, clusters and keywords.

C__________ [7]The analysis (*identify*) textual patterns, suggesting recurring associations between youth depression and suicide, and, to a lesser extent, alcohol use and bullying. [8]Keywords relating to emotional distress and symptoms of depression (*be*) less frequent. [9]A focus on the role of the parents (*be*) also evident.

D__________ [10]The analysis suggests that media coverage of depression in young people accurately reflects concerns reported in surveys by young people, but provides less information that might help in recognising depression in a young person.

7 Match headings 1–4 with sections A–D of Text 1. Compare your answers in pairs.

1 Conclusions
2 Objectives
3 Method
4 Results

Language focus

8 Work in pairs. Answer the questions about Text 1.

1 Why is the present simple used in sentence 1?
2 Which phrase in sentence 2 indicates that the present perfect should be used?
3 Why did the authors use the past simple for sentences 3 and 4?
4 Which verb form is used to describe the methods of research? Why?
5 Which tense would you use for the verbs in brackets in sentences 7, 8 and 9? Why?
6 How are the tenses in section D different from that of the previous section? Why?

9 Choose words and expressions in Text 1 that you could use when describing your own research, e.g. *a quantitative approach*.

10 Write 3–4 sentences about your research using words and expressions you have chosen in Activity 9. Use appropriate verb forms.

11 Work in pairs. Exchange your descriptions. Has your partner

- used appropriate verb forms?
- used the words/expressions correctly?

Reading

12 **Work in pairs. Put the headings for the sections of a good research article in the diagram. Compare your answers with another pair.**

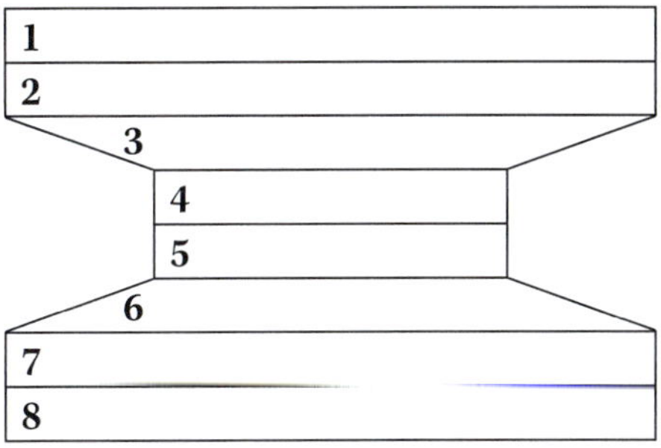

a References
b Discussion
c Title
d Materials and methods
e Introduction
f Results
g Conclusions
h Abstract

13 **Match the sections of a research article (a–h) in Activity 12 with their purposes (1–8).**

1 It summarises the research study and results of the study; it is included in article databases and is usually free to a large audience.
2 It describes both specific techniques and the overall experimental strategy used by researchers.
3 It clearly indicates the content of the article and helps interested readers to find the article quickly in a database.
4 It explains research findings and often deals with their applications.
5 It summarises the data collected and calculates totals or trends, statistically significant findings, etc.
6 It describes the theoretical background, indicates why the work is important, states a specific research question, and poses a specific hypothesis to be tested.
7 It states implications and recommends further research.
8 It lists the sources cited by the author(s) of the article.

14 **Identify which section of a research article statements 1–8 come from. Write *I* (Introduction), *M* (Materials and methods), *R* (Results) or *D* (Discussion) next to them. The first one has been done for you.**

1 We can suggest two reasons why some students persisted in their dislike of the technique. *D*
2 The search was limited to a five-year period from January 2007 to December 2011.
3 The frequency of use of the word 'children' is also noteworthy, considering that the search was targeted at reports concerning 'young people'. This suggests that children are increasingly being considered in discourse on depression and young people.
4 The average word length of the reports was 644.2 words (SD = 431.4)
5 All the articles were read and any article found not to be primarily about depression, specifically in young people, was excluded.
6 Despite great accessibility to information through the media, many people report difficulties finding relevant information on mental health.
7 Tables 2 and 3 highlight the frequent use of the words 'depression' and 'suicide' in the corpus.
8 Results suggest less emphasis in these Irish newspapers on the various symptoms (e.g. sleep problems, appetite issues) and treatment options available, which might make it difficult for parents to identify whether their child is depressed.

Speaking

15 **Work in groups. Discuss the questions and exchange your opinions with the whole class.**

1 Why does the article structure in Activity 12 have this kind of shape?
2 Is it a standard structure for research articles in your field?
3 Are there articles in your field with a structure different from the one in Activity 12? If so, how are they different?

Follow-up

16 **Find an article in your own language and an article from an English-medium journal, both related to your research area. Compare the format and structure of both articles and note down the differences, if there are any. Be ready to report your findings in the next class.**

Lesson 3 Titles and abstracts

Lead-in

1 Work in pairs. Discuss the questions.

1 When are you likely to write an abstract for an article: before you write your article, after you have written it or at the same time you write it? Why?
2 How long is an abstract in your field of research? What does its length depend on?
3 Which abstracts do you usually write: informative (they give the main results) or indicative (they only indicate what kind of research has been conducted)?

Reading

2 Read Text 1. Which of the kinds of information below does it include?

1 information about the specific place where the research was conducted
2 the number of surveys carried out
3 any negative results of the research project
4 a definition of the key term
5 information about different target groups
6 the need for further research
7 the practical implications of results

Text 1

[1]Reflection is a way of evaluating best practice and challenging existing norms, while at the same time considering our personal values and assumptions in our personal and professional lives. [2]However, many health practitioners may lack the skills to do this effectively. [3]Through participation in a series of three workshops, practitioners in the Radiation Medicine Programme at Princess Margaret Hospital have learned and acquired new skills [a]in order to encourage reflection and reflective practice in themselves and their colleagues as well as with their students. [4]A pre- and post-course survey was used [b]so that we could ascertain their level of knowledge of reflection and reflective practice. [5]An additional survey at 3 months assessed the frequency of use and ongoing comfort level with reflective practice. [6]Results of the evaluation indicate that the participants' knowledge of reflective practice has improved their understanding of reflection in clinical practice. [7]They recognise the importance of reflection and anticipate increasing their use of reflection in practice. [8]As well, participants have been able to sustain the positive momentum 3 months after the course was delivered.

ascertain: establish

anticipate: expect that something will happen

3 Compare Text 1 in Activity 2 with Text 1 in Activity 6 in Lesson 2 of this unit (see page 62). Tick the appropriate boxes in the table.

	Text 1 in Lesson 3	Text 1 in Lesson 2
1 The abstract is not longer than 200 words.		
2 The abstract contains background information.		
3 The abstract includes conclusions.		
4 Present tenses are used more than past tenses.		
5 Passive forms are frequently used.		

4 Identify the sentences (1–8) in Text 1 in Activity 2 that correspond to the elements of an abstract (a–e) below. Which element is not included in Text 1?

a background
b purpose of the study
c methodology of the study
d results
e conclusion or recommendation

Language focus

5 Read Text 2 and fill in the gaps with a suitable verb in the appropriate form.

Text 2

Grazing, or the uncontrolled, repetitive eating of small amounts of food [1] ________________ (*recognise/realise*) increasingly as an important eating behaviour associated with obesity. In spite of the need for a better understanding of this eating behaviour for improved obesity treatment, currently there is no empirically validated measure to [2] ________________ (*appreciate/assess*) grazing. Therefore, [c] to contribute to a better understanding of this relatively understudied eating pattern, a new self-report questionnaire of grazing [3] ________________ (*elaborate/develop*) in this study. Questionnaire items were designed [d] to reflect previous empirical descriptions of grazing. A group of 248 university students [4] ________________ (*complete/design*) the Grazing Questionnaire, other measures of eating-related behaviours and cognitions, and negative emotion. Sixty-two participants completed the Grazing Questionnaire a second time to calculate its temporal stability. Exploratory factor analysis [5] ________________ (*contain/reveal*) a clear two-factor solution for the questionnaire, reflecting repetitive eating behaviour and a perception of loss of control. Scores on the Grazing Questionnaire were positively associated with other measures of disordered eating, especially with binge eating. Initial psychometric properties of the new questionnaire are promising. Future research [6] ________________ (*need/want*) to examine the prevalence of this eating behaviour in more diverse populations, including those with binge eating disorder and obesity.

obesity: the state of being extremely fat

binge eating: eating too much at one time, especially without being able to control oneself

6 **Read the highlighted phrases a–d in Texts 1 and 2. Answer the questions below.**

1 Do these phrases express
   a cause? **b** effect? **c** purpose? **d** necessity?
2 Which structures are used in these phrases?
3 Where are these phrases placed in a sentence: before or after the main clause?
4 How does the structure of phrase b differ from the others?

Language Support: stating the purpose

In academic writing, research aims and objectives are commonly expressed with the help of infinitive phrases or clauses.

The aim of this study is/was to determine / to examine / to evaluate ...
To measure / To determine / To compare ..., ... was/were used.
In order to identify / to analyse / to understand ..., we ...
The experiment was conducted (in order) to find out ...
The survey was carried out so that we could discover ...

7 **Correct the mistakes in the sentences. Use the Language Support box to help you.**

1 For identify this metabolic product of yeast, glucose extracts were tested for their ability to stimulate acid secretion and gastrin release.
2 We tested children in pairs so that each child in the pair to observe visual illusions from different angles.
3 Laboratory experiments were carried out for us identifying the correlation between the two variables.
4 In order that we can investigate the effect of coffee consumption on hip fracture risk, a meta-analysis was conducted.
5 The purpose of this paper is proposing a model for the development of comprehensive assessments of older people and their carers.
6 For controlling these factors and investigating the relationship between risk and memory further, most of the remaining studies reported in this study use simulated driving in a laboratory setting.

Speaking

8 **Work in pairs. Match article titles 1–5 with the types of title a–e. More than one match may be possible.**

1 Mentoring Graduate Students in Teaching: The FCCIC Model
2 Encouraging Reflection: Do Professional Development Workshops Increase the Skill Level and Use of Reflection in Practice?
3 Creativity: A Review and Concept Analysis
4 Shifting the Goalposts: A Longitudinal Mixed-Methods Study of the Health of Long-Term Incapacity Benefit Recipients
5 Threats to the Running Water Ecosystems of the World

a titles that highlight a specific theme or focus following a general heading
b titles that emphasise the methodology used in the research
c titles that use rhetorical techniques (e.g. alliteration, allusion, metaphor)
d titles that contain a question
e titles that announce the general topic

9 **Work in pairs. Discuss what might be written in the articles under titles 1–4. Use the example to help you and the Language Support box.**

> **Language Support: expressing possibility**
> This article may focus on ...
> The purpose of the study might be ...
> In the introduction I might find ...
> The author(s) probably used (*methods*).
> The conclusions are likely to demonstrate that ...
> Perhaps/Maybe ...

1 Higher Education in Later Life: What is the Point?
2 Teaching More by Lecturing Less
3 Mind the Gap: Are Students Prepared for Higher Education?
4 Do Expectations Meet Reality? A Survey of Changes in First-Year Student Opinion

A: *What might the author mean by the question in the title?*
B: *Perhaps he or she considers why older people choose to do a university course.*
A: *What are you likely to find in the introduction to this article?*
B: *Well, it may be about ...*

Writing

10 **Think about an article you could write for an international journal. Write three or four titles of different types for it. Refer to Activity 8 for support.**

11 **Work in pairs. Read your partner's titles, identify their types and choose the best one. Use the criteria for conference titles in Activity 10 on page 17, which also apply to article titles.**

12 **Write a draft of your abstract (in 100–120 words). You can use the phrases below as support.**

- The present study investigates ______.
- We expected that ______.
- The method we applied involved ______.
- The results obtained show that ______.
- The study provides (strong) evidence that ______.

Follow-up

13 **Find three articles from your field of study on the internet. Analyse the article titles and complete the table.**

	1	2	3
1 How many words are used in the title?			
2 Is the title a noun phrase, a sentence or a question?			
3 Are nouns, adjectives and verbs capitalised?			
4 Are the keywords used in the title?			
5 Is it clear from the title what the article is about?			
6 Do you find this title appealing?			

Unit 2 Processing information

By the end of this unit you will be able to

- critically assess and discuss information found in book reviews
- analyse literature reviews in academic articles
- identify and use the vocabulary of evaluation
- use paraphrasing techniques
- write summaries of information from articles
- identify different citation styles
- write a list of references following standard conventions

Lesson 1 Book reviews

Lead-in

1 Work in pairs. Answer the questions.

1 Do you regularly read reviews of books in your field?
2 In which ways might they be useful to you?
3 Have you ever written a book review? Was it positive or negative?

2 Look at the cartoon. How would you describe this person?

3 Read the definitions in the table and complete the first column with the correct word from the list.

critic criticism critique

	n. the act of stating that something is bad or could be improved
	n. a report of something, such as a person's work or ideas, that examines it and provides a judgement of it
	n. 1 someone who says that they do not approve of someone or something **2** someone whose job is to give their opinion about something

Reading

4 Read the book review below (Text 1). Add the main points in it to the diagram. Compare your answers in pairs.

Text 1

***Learning and Talent Development*, by Jim Stewart and Clare Rigg, London, CIPD, 2011, 378 pp.**

This is a book written specifically for the latest qualifications and human resources (HR) competency framework of the Chartered Institute of Personnel and Development (CIPD). It has a useful table at the beginning illustrating which chapters meet which learning outcomes from the module of the same name as the book. This helps both teaching staff and students to navigate their way through the relevant reading.

Much of the philosophy and approach of the book is very explicitly explored in the short overview of the introduction. This is welcomed as it clearly indicates the authors' thinking regarding the purposes of this book, at least of the terms 'learning', 'talent development' and 'human resource development'. …

As with a previous book from the author Stewart, this book continues to maintain that easy-to-read style yet, at the same time drawing on a range of disciplines and often complex concepts. Tables are used to good effect to summarise ideas such as those of learning theory and learning styles. There are plenty of case illustrations and questions at the end of each chapter which can act as summarisers for the chapter or they can be developed into student-centred activities. The section on educational partnerships (part of Chapter 8), as it rightly states, is a growth area and one that is a foundation for many of the developments in work-based learning programmes. The critical questions within the chapter texts encourage readers to reflect on whether learning and development (L&D) practices or initiatives are always positive or 'good for' those who undertake them. …

The last chapter on student projects was an interesting digression into research approaches and methodologies. As it is written in the same very clear and thoughtful style it is a welcome addition to the many texts on undertaking research and being attached to a book of this nature helps to highlight the importance of sound research in all HR subject areas. However, as a personal preference, a chapter that addressed international differences in learning or educational experiences would have also added an extra dimension to the text. It would have widened its audience too, to international students who may well be keen to gain CIPD membership but also need to see their perspectives addressed more often. This would also support or enhance the final conclusions about the importance of understanding learning processes. In addition there seemed to be little reference to organisations other than CIPD, of which there are a number nationally and internationally involved with L&D/HRD – The University Forum for HRD and International Federation of Training Organisations, for example.

Despite the comments in the preceding paragraph, this is still a book that is very welcome, well worth the wait since the 1999 text by Stewart and coming with a successful collaborative co-authorship.

digression: movement away from the main subject you are writing or talking about

5 Work in pairs. Read Text 1 again and answer the questions.

1 Which positive feature is mentioned twice by the reviewer?
2 What kind of information does the reviewer put in brackets? Why does she put it in brackets?
3 Which other publications does the reviewer refer to?
4 Why is the last chapter of the book called 'a digression'?
5 Where in Text 1 does the reviewer refer to or mention herself?

6 Read Text 2. Compare it with Text 1. Say if Texts 1 and 2 are generally neutral, positive or negative.

Text 2

Families in Today's World: A Comparative Approach

David Cheal. London, England: Routledge. 2006. 172 pages.

... In the preface David Cheal states that the goal of his book is to provide an international textbook and a way of thinking about the family globally. Due to the increased focus on the impact of globalization and diversity on families, this is an admirable goal. Unfortunately, in practice this lofty goal is not achieved.

First, the basic format of the text is not conducive to student engagement with the reading. As a textbook, the reading has no charts, graphs, or photos, and does not utilize the traditional textbook format of sidebars. Additionally, the text does not provide questions for students to consider while reading, or definitions of terms within the chapters, which makes the book less than user-friendly for students and would necessitate extensive defining of terms during valuable class time.

Second, the absence of theory and traditional sociological terminology poses a problem for sociology of the family educators. There are no theories in this text. Theory is an important component of sociology which distinguishes it as a social science. The traditional family theories are not present, making this book difficult to use as a primary text for the sociology of the family.

Lastly and most importantly however, there are problems with the global focus in general. Our concerns about the global focus arise for four reasons: the western focus, the lack of comparisons across cultures, the omission of cultural discussions, and the limited cultural examples. ...

Because of the importance of global discussions in the teaching of the sociology of the family we regret that we do not have more positive feelings towards this text. One potential option for educators who wish to bring a more global perspective on families to the classroom would be to use this text as a supplement to their own lectures, bringing some of the global examples to highlight theories they discuss in class. We applaud the author's initiative to move towards a global view of families and hope that this path is continued upon. However, simply put, this book provides neither the solid foundation expected of a primary text nor the engagement and story to be a supplementary reading text.

7 Compare the books reviewed in Texts 1 and 2. Complete the table.

	Learning and Talent Development	*Families in Today's World: A Comparative Approach*
Type		
Application		
Readership		
Features of contents		
Features of structure		

Language focus

8 Underline the phrases in Texts 1 and 2 which helped you decide on the reviewers' attitudes to the books reviewed.

9 Look at the highlighted adverbs in each text. What is their function?

10 Read the Language Support box below. Which two adverbs from Texts 1 and 2 can be added to it?

> **Language Support: sentence adverbs**
>
> Sentence adverbs allow writers to express their opinion indirectly, without mentioning themselves. A sentence adverb often starts a sentence and is followed by a comma.
>
> Examples of sentence adverbs are: interestingly (enough), (not) surprisingly, obviously, supposedly, presumably, seemingly, ____________, ____________.

11 Here is part of Text 1 again. What makes it different from the rest of the review?

> However, as a personal preference, a chapter that addressed international differences in learning or educational experiences would have also added an extra dimension to the text. It would have widened its audience too, to international students who may well be keen to gain CIPD membership but also need to see their perspectives addressed more often. This would also support or enhance the final conclusions about the importance of understanding learning processes. In addition there seemed to be little reference to organisations other than CIPD, of which there are a number nationally and internationally involved with LD/HRD …

12 Add six examples from the passage in Activity 11 to the Language Support box.

> **Language Support: hedging**
>
> Hedging is the use of cautious language – a feature of academic writing which involves making one's statements less categorical or assertive.
>
> - **verbs:** believe, suggest, think, ____________
> - **some modal verbs:** can, could, might, ____________, ____________
> - **use of comparative forms:** more acceptable (instead of *acceptable*), more common, ____________
> - **use of** ____________ **and** ***few*** instead of *no, none, nothing*
> - **use of qualifying adjectives or adverbs:** fairly, quite, slightly, almost, practically, etc.
> - **modifying phrases:** from my point of view, some might say ..., one angle on this might be ... ____________

13 **Read part of an article review written by a sociology student. Use the hedging techniques from the Language Support box to improve it.**

Professional skills and ethics, which so far have attracted no attention, are analysed in this article from a narrow perspective, which focuses on the job of an economist. However, the conclusions of the author apply to any profession. The pace of development in society is fast in all spheres of life, which creates a new system of standards and requirements. Thus, professionalism comes to be viewed through the lens of morality, which is a complex notion, difficult to define objectively. It is really impossible to use morality as a criterion in assessing the degree of professionalism of any employee.

Speaking

14 **Work in pairs. Follow the steps below.**

1 Think of a book or article in your professional field.
2 Prepare to describe it to your colleague. Use the Language Support boxes and the phrases you underlined in Activity 8.
3 Take turns to briefly describe the book or article and your opinion of it.
4 Ask each other questions about your reviews.

Follow-up

15 **Find on the internet two reviews of books in your area of specialism. Focus on both language and content and answer the questions below. Make notes on your findings and report them to the whole class.**

1 What features do these reviews have in common with the reviews in this lesson?
2 In what way(s) are they different?

Lesson 2 Literature reviews

Lead-in

1 Answer the questions.

1 Where in a journal article can you often find references to other authors' work?
2 Where are they unlikely to appear? Why?

Reading

2 Work in pairs. Look through Text 1 and guess the meaning of the highlighted words without using a dictionary. Be ready to report what helped you: the context, a similar word in your own language, association with another word with the same root or something else.

Text 1

Uncontrolled, Repetitive Eating of Small Amounts of Food or 'Grazing': Development and Evaluation of a New Measure of Atypical Eating

The increasing prevalence of obesity and associated health risks is a concern in many societies. Nevertheless, relatively little is known about the atypical or disordered eating patterns that may be associated with overweight and obesity (Carter & Jansen, 2012). Eating behaviours contributing to obesity appear to be heterogeneous, and many of them are not included among the criteria that define eating disorders in the *Diagnostic and Statistical Manual of Mental Disorders* (DSMIV- TR; American Psychiatric Association [APA], 2000). Descriptions of atypical eating behaviours associated with overweight and obesity include 'binge eating' (e.g., Darby, Hay, Mond, Rodgers & Owen, 2007), 'constant overeating' (Mitchell, Devlin, de Zwaan, Crow, & Peterson, 2008), 'picking' (Fairburn, 2008), 'grazing' (Saunders, 2004), 'betweenmeal snacking' (O'Connor, Jones, Connor, McMillan, & Ferguson, 2008), 'night eating' (Colles, Dixon, & O'Brien, 2007), and a general 'chaotic' and unstructured eating style (Hagan, Whitworth, & Moss, 1999). To date, binge eating has received the greatest amount of research attention among these overeating behaviours. The proposed diagnosis of Binge Eating Disorder (BED) in DSM-IV (APA, 2000) is defined by the presence of discrete binge-eating episodes that are characterised by an unusually large intake of food in a single sitting. These episodes are accompanied by a sense of a lack of control over eating, behavioural manifestations of a lack of control, and emotional distress. ...

3 Read Text 1 again and divide it into two paragraphs. Explain what helped you to decide where to divide it.

4 Work in pairs. Answer the questions about Text 1.

1 How do the authors state that their research is topical?
2 Why are the different kinds of atypical eating behaviours given here?
3 Which atypical eating behaviour do the authors choose to define in the text?
4 Is the defined atypical eating behaviour the focus of the article?

5 Decide which of the sentences below best summarises Text 1.

1 There are a lot of eating behaviours associated with obesity, many of which are not necessarily known or treated as eating disorders, unlike binge eating, which has been extensively studied.
2 Numerous attempts have been made to study obesity and the health risks connected with various eating behaviours, among which binge eating is the most researched.

6 Read Text 2. Match the highlighted words with their definitions (1–4).

1 long life
2 emotion
3 including different types of things
4 a person's husband or wife

Text 2

Emmons and Crumpler (2000) describe gratitude as a multifaceted relational concept encompassing emotion, attitude, behaviour and motivation. Focusing on emotion, Lazarus and Lazarus (1994) describe feelings of gratitude as the result of '*appreciating* an *altruistic* gift' (p. 118, emphasis in original) and highlight its relational context. Thus, feelings of gratitude arise from a perception that another person's actions are the reason for some benefit to oneself, and an appreciation of those actions and of the one responsible for them.

In a study of the effects of reflecting on experiences of gratitude, Emmons and McCullough (2003) reported increases in positive affect and life satisfaction and that these changes were also observed by participants' spouses or significant others. In a study exploring gratitude in marital relationships, Mikulincer et al. (2006, p. 209) concluded that gratitude contributes 'strength and longevity to romantic and marital relationships'. These findings suggest not only that the personal benefits of being grateful toward one's romantic partner are apparent to one's romantic partner but that being grateful also benefits one's romantic relationship.

7 Read Text 2 again. Say which words could be included in the title of this article.

Language focus

8 Complete the table with nouns corresponding to each verb. Compare your answers in pairs. If in doubt, consult a dictionary.

Verbs	Nouns
appreciate	*appreciation*
perceive	
contribute	
suggest	
explore	
observe	
reflect	

9 **Fill in the gaps with a noun or a verb from Activity 8.**

1 Of special interest is students' ______________ of science and scientists: is their view of science, like the scientists' view of humanities, limited?
2 In its time, the French Revolution made an enormous ______________ to human progress.
3 Newcomers bring their own interests and beliefs into the community, and they do not ______________ or recognise the value of agricultural work.
4 The conclusions are based on empirical ______________ ; most women and older children are actually quite as rational as most men while some men are actually less rational.
5 Measures of poverty which are based on the family or the household as the unit of measurement cannot accurately ______________ the true extent of poverty among women.
6 There is the ______________ that organic molecules arose elsewhere in the Universe, perhaps on dust particles in space, and were first carried to Earth on meteorites.

10 **Read Text 2 again.**

1 Write down the 'reporting verbs'. They are often used in summaries.
2 Which of the following verbs also belong to this group?
increase emphasise provide claim argue
perform indicate state conduct consider

11 **Compare this paraphrase with the original text. Which techniques in the Language Support box has the writer used to produce the paraphrase?**

Paraphrase: The importance of Information and Communication Technology (ICT) as a tool in developing English language learners' communicative competence can hardly be overestimated.

Original: There is hardly anyone who would question the fact that Information and Communication Technology (ICT) plays an important role in developing the skills and knowledge learners need to communicate effectively in the English language.

Language Support: paraphrasing and summarising

A literature review is a brief overview of what has been written on your topic. In it you summarise other authors' ideas – you present them in a condensed form. To do this effectively, without plagiarising*, you need to paraphrase.

Paraphrasing is describing the ideas of others in your own words. When paraphrasing, you can

- use only the key words of the original
- use words similar in meaning to those of the original text
- change parts of speech, e.g. *agree* > *agreement*
- change the order of words or sentences
- use grammatical structures and vocabulary which are different from those in the original
- combine sentences.

*plagiarising – using ideas and/or words from other authors' works without acknowledging the source.

12 **Write paraphrases of the following extracts. Use the guidelines from the Language Support box and reporting verbs from Activity 10.**

> **Tip:**
> Don't forget to use the authors' names in your paraphrases.

A

> One potential option for educators who wish to bring a more global perspective on families to the classroom would be to use this text as a supplement to their own lectures bringing some of the global examples to highlight theories they discuss in class. (P.R. Koch, D.H. Swanson)

B

> The analysis of recently published course books revealed that the majority of their authors tend to overlook the potential of the Internet in teaching specialist English. Such materials fail to respond in this respect to the requirements of the modern world of study and work. (L.B. Smith, I.Y. Sheml)

C

> Although many students in the S'04 and S'05 courses at first disliked and distrusted the interactive classes and group activities, most became comfortable with the unfamiliar format and ultimately reported that it helped their learning. Some students, however, never fully accepted the new approaches. (J.K. Knight, W.B. Wood)

13 **Write a one-sentence summary of Text 2 (as in Activity 5).**

14 **Work in pairs. Compare your paraphrases and summaries, and choose the best ones, using the criteria below.**

The paraphrase

- contains the key words from the original
- is no longer, and is ideally shorter, than the original
- uses different grammatical structures from those in the original
- accurately expresses the information given in the original
- uses adequate substitutes for the vocabulary of the original
- contains a reference to the source (the author).

Follow-up

15 Choose a paragraph from an article you would like to refer to. Write a summary of the paragraph for the Literature Review section. Use the guidelines from the Language Support box and Activity 14.

Important: Keep your summary. You will use it to write an Introduction in Unit 3.

Lesson 3 Citations and references

Lead-in

1 Work in pairs. Complete the words with verbs or nouns describing what authors usually do when reporting other researchers' findings.

1 _ _ _ _ _ R _ _ _
2 _ _ _ E
3 P _ _ _ _ _ _ _ _ _
4 _ O _ _ _ _ _
5 R _ _ _ _ _ _ _ _
6 _ _ _ T _ _ _ _

1 to express the most important facts or ideas about something in a short and clear form
2 to speak or write words taken from a particular writer or written work
3 to repeat something written or spoken using different words
4 to express an opinion about something; something that you say or write that expresses your opinion
5 the act of mentioning someone or something in speech or writing
6 to review or discuss critically ; a report of something, such as a person's work or ideas, that examines it and provides a judgement of it

Reading

2 Read Text 1 and sentences A–D. These are the first and last sentences of the paragraphs in Text 1. Find the two topic sentences (general statements introducing the main idea of the paragraph) and write the correct letters in gaps 1 and 3. Then decide where the concluding sentences fit in.

Text 1

1 ______ These outcomes are obtained through the conscious act of thinking about past events, attending to the feelings and ideas that arise from those events and visualizing the resultant change[4]. These actions are echoed in Kolb's theory of experiential learning. Both processes involve observing a situation, realizing that one is in a situation, thinking about it and then making decisions about what to do next[5–7]. 2 ______

3 ______ A practitioner who is self-aware and reflective in their work is more likely to be able to develop good critical self-appraisal and clinical reasoning skills[7,9,10]. They would be able to engage in continual evaluation of their professional practice, critically analyzing and developing it further[11–14] and be able to narrow the theory–practice gap by reflecting on their experience[7,9,11,14–17]. This would lead to practitioners developing greater self-awareness, confidence

> and understanding[1,9,13–16]. Structured reflective learning activities could assist practitioners to appreciate their practice knowledge, and understand and value their experiences more fully. 4 ________

A This can empower practitioners to own their knowledge, contribute more fully[1,18], and thus impact positively on changing clinical practice[13,19].
B At the core of the reflective process is the acquiring of new understanding and appreciation, by reframing problems and through the development of knowledge creation capacities[3].
C Reflection is also an important component of critical thinking.
D They are all essential steps in the learning process[8].

3 Read Text 1 and answer the questions.

1 Which paragraph expresses an opinion? What helped you to decide?
2 What is the function of the other paragraph: to compare and contrast, to provide arguments, to present an analysis of a concept, to persuade?
3 In which paragraph does the concluding sentence present an argument?
4 Which words in the first paragraph serve to summarise details or to summarise what is written earlier in the text?

4 Write a one-sentence summary of Text 1. For an example, see Activity 5 on page 76.

Tip:
To start, highlight the key words that will go into the summary.

Language focus

5 Match the words and phrases below with the highlighted words and phrases in Text 1, which are similar in meaning. Which set of words is more formal?

1 to acknowledge ________
2 help ________
3 part ________
4 looking at ________
5 to take part in ________
6 repeated ________
7 getting ________

6 **Read the Language Support box. Fill in the gaps in the text below with either a noun or a gerund formed from the verbs in brackets.**

> **Language Support: gerunds**
>
> A gerund is formed by adding *-ing* to the verb. It is a verb form that functions in sentences like a noun. It is often used in academic writing to describe actions, states and processes. Note that after *the -ing, of* is used before another noun.
> Compare:
> *Writing a research article is difficult at first, but it gets easier with practice.*
> *The writing of a research article requires careful planning and adherence to certain conventions.*
>
> A noun is preferred to a gerund when it describes a thing, event or quality, or when it follows a possessive adjective.
> *The introduction to the book is concise and well written.*
> *Their decision to investigate the issue was strange.* (This is better than: *Their deciding to investigate ...*)

[1]__________ *(refer)* to information from another source can be done in several ways. Writers can do this by [2]__________ *(quote)* directly from the original publication or by [3]__________ *(rephrase)* it in their own words. [4]__________ *(paraphrase)* original sources is a skill in itself and involves [5]__________ *(use)* as few words from the original as possible and [6]__________ *(change)* the rest of the language from the cited source. However, the meaning of the [7]__________ *(cite)* should stay unchanged though [8]__________ *(shorten)* the original is possible. By [9]__________ *(cite)* sources we demonstrate our [10]__________ *(know)* of the work done by other researchers.

Reading

7 **Read Text 2 and answer the questions.**

1 What is its main similarity to Text 1?
2 Apart from the contents, what is its major difference from Text 1?

Text 2

> [1]The concept of gratitude has received recent research attention (e.g., Lambert, Graham, & Fincham, 2009; McCullough & Tsang, 2004; Mikulincer & Shaver, 2010). [2]However, despite Emmons and Crumpler's (2000, p. 57) assertion that 'gratitude is profoundly interpersonal', the role of gratitude in romantic relationships has, to date, received little research attention (Emmons, 2004; Hlava, 2009). [3]Although few studies have explored gratitude in romantic relationships, Mikulincer et al. (2006) have identified an association in romantic couples between gratitude and some aspects of attachment and found that individuals who were higher in gratitude and more secure in some aspects of attachment were more likely to engage in prosocial behaviour.

8 Read the Language Support box. Say which sentences, or parts of sentences, in Text 2 are information-prominent and which are author-prominent. Give reasons.

Language Support: information-prominent and author-prominent writing

In the description of other authors' work the primary focus may be on the information/findings or on the researcher(s). Accordingly, in the first case – an information-prominent text – the names of the researchers would be in parentheses; in the second case, they would be subjects in author-prominent clauses or sentences.

9 Read the Language Support box and say which citation styles are used in Text 1 and Text 2.

Language Support: citation styles

The **Harvard Style** of citing sources is often referred to as the author-date method, which applies to in-text citations, e.g. *(Harper 2004), (Smith 1997, p. 82), (Carter & Jansen 2009).* Reference list entries are given alphabetically by the author's surname.

The **American Psychological Association (APA)** citation style is often used in social sciences. It is slightly different from the Harvard Style. In-text references contain the author's name, the year of publication and, if necessary, the page in the original source. *(Simms, 2011); Dunning T (1993).*
The list of references is in alphabetical order.

The **Vancouver** citation style is used to refer to sources in medicine, health sciences, etc. In-text citations are marked with numbers in superscript, e.g. *Some studies [6-11, 15] have examined the effect of air pollution in urban areas.* Apart from numbers, in-text citations contain no other information about the sources. Items are included in the list of references in the order they appear in the text

10 Work in pairs. Read extracts from reference lists from two articles and write down the different types of sources they contain, e.g. a journal article, and the order in which information is given in the reference. Student A analyses List A, Student B – List B. Compare your notes. Discuss the differences in style.

A

References

1. Newnham J. To reflect or not? Reflective practice in radiation therapy. *Journal of Radiotherapy in Practice* 1999; 1:109-116.
2. Radiation Medicine Program. Professional Practice Model. http://intranet.rmp.uhn.on.ca. Accessed 9 March 2011.
3. Williams GR, Lowes L. Reflection: possible strategies to improve its use by qualified staff. *British Journal of Nursing* 2001; 10:1482-1488.
4. Newell R. Anxiety, accuracy and reflection: the limits of professional development. *Journal of Advanced Nursing* 1992; 17:1326-1333.
5. Bolton G. *Reflective Practice: Writing and Professional Development.* London: Paul Chapman, 2001.

B

10. Hlava, P. (2009). *Exploring the lived experience of gratitude in couple relationships.* (Unpublished doctoral thesis). Institute of Transpersonal Psychology, Palo Alto, CA.
11.Lazarus, R.S., & Lazarus, B.N. (1994). *Passion and Reason: Making Sense of Our Emotions.* New York: Oxford University Press.
12. McCullough, M.E., Emmons, R.A., & Tsang, J.-A. (2001). *The Gratitude Questionnaire —six item* form (GQ-6) Retrieved from http://www.psy.miami.edu/faculty/mmccullough/ gratitude/2Page%20Blurb%20on%20the%20Gratitude%20Questionnaire.pdf
14. McCullough, M.E., Kilpatrick, S.D., Emmons, R.A., & Larson, D.B. (2001). Is gratitude a moral affect? *Psychological Bulletin,* 127, 249–266.
15. Prager, K.J. (1995). *The Psychology of Intimacy.* New York: Guilford Press.
16. Reis, H.T., & Shaver, P. (1988). Intimacy as an interpersonal process. In S. Duck, D.F. Hay, S.E. Hobfoll, W. Ickes & B.M. Montgomery (Eds.), *Handbook of Personal Relationships: Theory, Research and Interventions.* (pp. 367–389). Oxford, England: John Wiley & Sons.

Writing

11 Study the authors' guidelines for the journal in which you would like to publish your paper (see Activity 15 on page 58). Make a reference list for your article. Follow the recommendations on referencing.

12 Work in pairs. Exchange your reference lists. Identify the referencing style used by your partner. Check it for consistency.

Follow-up

13 Compare citation and referencing norms in your country and in the English-speaking world. Check if the examples you have found follow the conventions described above. Report your findings to the whole class.

Unit 3 Describing research

By the end of this unit you will be able to
- structure the Introduction section of a research article
- use appropriate language to indicate a gap in your field of research
- describe the methods and materials used in your research
- refer to visuals in your article
- write a draft description of your research results, highlighting the main results

Lesson 1 Introductions

Lead-in

1 Work in pairs. Discuss the questions.

1 Do you find writing the Introduction section of an academic article easy or difficult? Why?
2 What is the main purpose of the Introduction section?
3 What kind of information do you always include in this section?

Reading

2 Text 1 describes five main stages that often appear in Introductions (after Weisseberg & Buker 1990, p. 22; Cargill & O'Connor 2009, p. 42). Fill in the gaps with the words in the box.

centrality	context	findings	niche	objectives	researchers	value

Text 1

Stage 1. Statements about the field of research to provide the reader with a setting or 1 __________ for the problem to be investigated and to claim its 2 __________ or importance.
Stage 2. More specific statements about the aspects of the problem already studied by other 3 __________ , laying a foundation of information already known.
Stage 3. Statements that indicate the need for more investigation, creating a gap or research 4 __________ for the present study to fill.
Stage 4. Statements giving the 5 __________ of the writer's study or outlining its main activity or 6 __________ .
Stage 5. Statements that give a positive 7 __________ or justification for carrying out the study.

3 Text 2 is an Introduction whose parts (A–E) are jumbled up. Put the parts into a logical order and then match them with the stages in Text 1. Compare your answers in pairs.

Text 2

______ A There is now a great deal of evidence that lecturing is a relatively ineffective pedagogical tool for promoting conceptual understanding. Some of this evidence is general, showing that learners gain meaningful understanding of concepts primarily through active engagement with and application of new information, not by passive listening to verbal presentations (reviewed in National Research Council, 1999). More specific evidence shows that students learn substantially more from active inquiry-based activities and problem solving than from listening to lectures (Beichner and Saul, 2003).

_____ B To address the validity of these concerns, we carried out an experiment in "scientific teaching" (Handelsman et al., 2004) in a large upper-level Developmental Biology course, in which the same two instructors, teaching the same syllabus, tested the effect of two different teaching styles on student learning gains in successive semesters.

_____ C Thirty years ago, the future success of biology students might have been predictable by the amount of factual knowledge they had accumulated in their college courses. Today, there is much more information to learn, but the increasingly easy accessibility of facts on the Internet is making long-term memorization of details less and less important. Therefore, teaching for conceptual understanding and analytical skills while encouraging collaborative activities makes increasing sense in undergraduate courses.

_____ D The results we present here indicate that even a moderate shift toward more interactive and cooperative learning in class can result in significantly higher student learning gains than achieved using a standard lecture format.

_____ E Nevertheless, many university faculty who are comfortable with their lecture courses remain unconvinced that more interactive teaching will lead to increased student learning, or that interactive teaching is even feasible in large classes.

4 **Find the title below which is NOT suitable for the article with this Introduction (Text 2). Which do you think the original title is? Why?**

a Changing the Course Format Leads to Higher Student Learning Gains
b Teaching More by Lecturing Less
c The Impact of Lecturing on Student Learning
d Interactivity: an Experiment in 'Scientific Teaching'

Language focus

5 **In Text 2 underline words and expressions which helped you to identify each stage described in Text 1.**

6 **Start writing Stage 1 of the Introduction to your article. Write three sentences describing the context for the summary you wrote for your Literature Review section (see Activity 15 on page 79). Use expressions from Text 2. Follow the pattern: area → subarea → topic.**

7 **Text 3 is an extract from the Introduction to the article 'The Development of Researchers' Communicative Competence'. Read it and identify the stage it is (as described in Text 1). Fill in the gaps with the linking words and phrase below.**

Although	Despite	In addition

Text 3

[1] _____ the dissemination of Bologna ideas in Europe, communication between researchers is still restricted due to their insufficient level of English. Most studies in the field of language teaching have only focused on developing linguistic competence rather than communicative ability to interact with professionals in particular environments. [2] _____, little attention has been paid to developing learners' subcompetences such as pragmatic and discursive ones. This indicates a need to understand the mechanisms underlying the integration of all subcompetences including cross-cultural communication. [3] _____ several attempts have been made to design teaching materials for researchers (Yakhontova, 2003), very few studies have investigated the impact of teaching materials on raising learners' language awareness in general.

8 Read the Language Support box and complete it with expressions from Text 3.

Language Support: indicating the gap

Adjectives
Nevertheless, the attempts to ... are/remain at present controversial/incomplete/questionable/unsatisfactory.

Verbs
However, previous research has failed to ... / ignored ... / misinterpreted ... / underestimated ...

Nouns
There is a gap in /________________ / a demand for ...

Negative openings
However, little information/________________ /data/research/work ...
Despite ... /Although ... , few investigations /________________ / researchers ...
No studies/data/calculations/findings have shown/demonstrated ...
____

Writing

9 Continue writing your Introduction with 3–5 statements, indicating the gap in your field of research.

10 Exchange your drafts. Check if your partner has

- convinced you that the problem is topical
- referred to other researchers in the field
- clearly indicated the gap
- divided the text into paragraphs appropriately
- developed the text logically
- used words and expressions from Text 2 (see Activity 5) and the Language Support box
- avoided grammar and spelling mistakes.

Give feedback to your partner.

11 Redraft your Introduction, taking into account your partner's feedback.

Follow-up

12 On the internet find an article in your specialism. Read the Introduction and identify Stage 4 (the objectives of the study and/or its main findings) and Stage 5 (the positive value of the research). Write out key phrases indicating these stages. Prepare two slides to share in class.

13 Discuss your findings with the whole class.

Lesson 2 Method and process

Lead-in

1 Read the quotation and discuss to what extent it is true in your specialist field.

We have to remember that what we observe is not nature in itself but nature exposed to our method of questioning. (Werner Heisenberg)

2 Work in pairs. Discuss the questions.

1 How can the Method section of an article be helpful for researchers?
2 What other names for this section are used in journals from your field?

Reading

3 Text 1 is part of the Method section of the article 'Media representation of depression in young people: a corpus-based analysis of Irish newspaper coverage'. Match sentences 1–12 in the text with the elements of the Method section they present (a–e). The same sentence may be matched with more than one element.

a an overview of the research
b materials
c sample
d procedures
e location

sample: a group of people or things that is chosen out of a larger number and is asked questions or tested in order to get information about the larger group

Text 1

[1]The current study examined Irish newspaper accounts of depression in young people, focusing on broadsheet publications between the years 2007 and 2011. [2]Newspaper articles concerning depression in young people were located online using the LexisNexis News & Business database, ProQuest and the Irish News Archives databases. [3]The search terms were 'depression' or 'depressed' or 'mental health' and 'youth' or 'young people'. [4]The search query was limited to the three traditional broadsheet newspapers: *The Irish Times*, *The Irish Independent* and *The Examiner*.

[5]The resulting 269 newspaper articles, containing 176 223 words, were analysed using WordSmith™ Tools (Scott, 2008), a program used for counting word frequencies, finding word patterns and identifying keywords. [6]WordSmith™ was initially used to compile a word list on the basis of frequency. [7]This stage is useful to examine the vocabulary used in the texts.

[8]In the second stage of the analysis, keywords were identified by analysing the content in comparison with a reference corpus. [9]The significance of the difference in frequency between the word in the word list and in the reference corpus is calculated statistically using log-likelihood tests (Dunning, 1993). [10]Keywords can then be grouped according to specific topics. [11]We used the British National Corpus (BNC), a 100 million word collection of samples of mainly (90%) written language taken from a wide variety of sources. [12]Finally, textual patterns were explored in the context of word clusters (such as patterns of repeated phraseology) and collocates (i.e. other words that tend to occur in the neighbourhood of the search word).

log-likelihood: a type of statistical test

4 **Work in pairs. Discuss the questions about Text 1.**

1 Which method was used by the researchers?
2 Which materials were examined?
3 How many procedural stages were completed by the authors? Which phrases helped you to identify them?
4 Which elements do you think are always included in the Method section of research articles?
5 Do you find this procedural description clear? Would you be able to replicate this experiment? Why? / Why not?

Language focus

5 **Read Text 1 again. Answer the questions.**

1 Which tense is used most frequently in Text 1? Why?
2 Which sentences are written in the present simple tense? Why?
3 Which verbs are used in the passive voice? Why?
4 Which sentences are written in the active voice? Why?

6 **Read Text 1 again. Focus on the highlighted verb+*ing* forms. Discuss the questions.**

1 Which of the verb+*ing* forms describe how the authors did their research?
2 Which of them describes how the authors found something? Which preposition is used with the verb+*ing* form?
3 Which of them show the purpose of a tool? Which preposition is used with the verb+*ing* form?

> **Language Support: verb+*ing* for gerunds and present participles**
>
> The verb form verb +*ing* can be used for gerunds, which function as nouns (see page 82). Gerunds can be used after a preposition, e.g.
> *Before submitting your article, please read the author guidelines carefully.*
> *I can't respond to your request without discussing it first with my colleagues.*
>
> Verb +*ing* is also used for present participles. These can be used like adverbs, e.g.
> *We have been researching depression for five years, looking at what can cause it.*
> *The authors of this paper explain their concepts clearly, giving many relevant examples.*

Listening

7 **Work in pairs. Discuss which equipment or other materials you use to carry out your research. Specify if necessary.**

1 laboratory equipment
2 natural substances
3 surveys, questionnaires, tests
4 computer models/programmes
5 mathematical models
6 human and animal subjects

8 25 **Listen to a tutor explaining how to write the Materials section of an article. Say what he finds essential and why.**

Reading and Writing

9 Read Text 2 about the eating behaviour 'grazing' (see page 66) and match the subheadings (1–3) with parts of the Method section (A–C).

1 Materials **2** Procedure **3** Participants

Text 2

A ____________________

A group of 248 undergraduate psychology students (73% women) [1] ____________________ (*take part*) in the study after volunteering via a standard university-based participant recruitment website. The majority of the participants reported being single (n = 148, 59.7%) or in a dating relationship without living together (n = 85, 34.3%). The participants' relevant health characteristics were assessed by [2] ____________________ (*measure*) height and weight and [3] ____________________ (*ask*) participants to report on factors that could influence weight status.

B ____________________

Body Mass Index (BMI) [4] ____________________ (*calculate*) from objective height and weight measurements and [5] ____________________ (*categorise*) according to World Health Organization guidelines (WHO, 1998). According to WHO classifications, a BMI under 18.5 is 'underweight' and BMI greater than 30 is defined as 'obese'. In addition, a brief Grazing Questionnaire (GQ) [6] ____________________ (*develop*) by the authors for the current study. Eight new items [7] ____________________ (*create*) to measure behaviours and cognitions specific to grazing. Scores are summed to form a total score (range: 0–32), where higher scores [8] ____________________ (*represent*) more grazing behaviours and cognitions.

C ____________________

Initially, the study protocol [9] ____________________ (*approve*) by the relevant institutional ethics committee. Then students [10] ____________________ (*volunteer*) for participation via an online recruitment system. Objective height and weight measurements [11] ____________________ (*take*) at the beginning of data collection. Participants [12] ____________________ (*ask*) to stand on the scales without shoes and other weight-bearing items (coats, keys). Height was measured [13] ____________________ (*use*) a tape measure affixed to the wall. Following these measurements, participants [14] ____________________ (*complete*) a Grazing Questionnaire (GQ). To calculate temporal stability, a subgroup of students (n = 74) was randomly selected and asked to complete the Grazing Questionnaire a second time, 7 days after the initial data collection took place. Of this group, 62 individuals [15] ____________________ (*return*) the completed questionnaires via email (83.8% response rate), between 7 and 62 days following the first data collection session.

ethics committee: a committee which checks that the research conducted is ethical

10 In Text 2 fill in the gaps with the appropriate verb form: the present or past simple in the active or passive or verb+*ing*.

11 Work in pairs. Discuss the questions.

1 How were participants selected for the study?
2 Which materials were investigated?
3 Which methods were used?
4 How many steps were undertaken by the authors? Which words signal each step?

12 Add examples from Text 2 to the Language Support box.

Language Support: sequencing

First/Initially ... ______________________________
Prior to completing the questionnaire, all students were informed of ...
Secondly/Next/Subsequently/Later ... ______________________________
After collection, the samples were analysed ... ______________________________
Following this, the data were ... ______________________________
Finally/Lastly, questions were asked to ...

13 Choose the right words or phrases in Text 3 to complete the procedure part of the Method section in the article 'Being Grateful: Does It Make Us Closer? Gratitude, Attachment and Intimacy in Romantic Relationships'. Compare answers in pairs.

Text 3

This study included both an Australian university student sample and a community [1]*sample/subject*. [2]*Eventually/Initially*, participants [3]*were recruited/recruited* via advertisements placed on university noticeboards and through snowballing techniques [4]*used/using* the researchers' networks of colleagues and acquaintances. Data collection [5]*was conducted/was measured* online. [6]*Following/Prior to* standard ethics procedures, participants [7]*completed/were completed* the questionnaire online in their own time. [8]*Unexpectedly/Lastly*, a proportion of the university [9]*staff/students* were eligible for course credit as a result of their participation.

Follow-up

14 Read the Method section of an article from your field of study. Find and copy out the information below.

1 what was investigated
2 which methods were used
3 which materials were used
4 which steps and procedures were undertaken

15 Make a list similar to that in Activity 14 based on your own research. Write a draft of the Method section of your article. Self-check it answering the questions below.
Have you used

- the active and passive voice appropriately?
- the verb+*ing* form to show how you carried out your research?
- the verb+*ing* form to explain the purpose of each tool (material)?
- sequencing words to show the steps followed?
- a formal style?

Lesson 3 Results

Lead-in

1 Read the statement and fill in the gaps with the words *Results* or *Discussion*. Say if you agree with the statement.

Separating [1] ______________ from [2] ______________ preserves the objectivity of the [3] ______________ which should be presented clearly and without comment. (D. Lindsay)

Writing

2 Put the words in the correct order to make sentences about the Results section of an article.

1 provide evidence / in a research article / aims to / or reject / to support / a hypothesis. / The data presentation

____

2 most prominent. / We should / the main points / present / in ways which / make / all necessary data

____

3 to focus on / to interpret them. / helps readers / aspects of / and / the results / The accompanying text / the least important

____

4 should / randomly / Figures / and put / be numbered / in the article.

____

5 in the text. / Figures / in the order / referred to / are presented / in which they / should be

____

6 depends on what / to gain from your data. / a table, graph, diagram or text / The choice of / you want readers / whether to use

____

3 Work in pairs. Compare your sentences and decide whether they are true or false.

Reading and Speaking

4 Look at the table from the Results section of the article 'Teaching More by Lecturing Less' (the Introduction to which is on pages 85–6). Work in pairs and discuss the questions.

1 Why are the two groups of results (Fall '03, Spring '04) presented?
2 Which column do you think shows the results of the interactive course?
3 Which results in the table would you expect the article to refer to particularly?

Table 4. Comparison of average performance on different assessments for the two courses

Assessment	Performance (average percent of maximum score)	
	Fall 2003	Spring 2004
Pre-test (12 questions)[a]	34	31
Post-test (12 questions)[a]	65	74
Normalized learning gain[b]	46	62
Final exam	77	71
Problem sets	82	85
Participation	N/A	86
Final total points	76	81

a Data based only on the 12 questions that were common to all three pre-tests and post-tests.
b Average for each class is shown.

5 Text 1 is an extract from the Results section which describes the table in Activity 4. Read it and check if your answers to question 3 in Activity 4 were correct.

Text 1

[1]As shown in Table 4, the average performance on exams and problem sets differed only slightly between the two semesters. [2]Although the questions on the F'03 and S'04 exams were similar, they were not identical. [3]The exams in S'04 were designed to test more conceptual and less factual knowledge than those in F'03. [4]Because the exams were substantially different, we cannot make meaningful comparisons of exam performances between the two semesters. [5]The average performance and standard deviation on the pre-test were not significantly different in the two semesters: traditional, 34% (±12%); interactive, 31% (±12%), indicating that the incoming students were equally well prepared. [6]However, the average performance on the post-test was significantly higher in the interactive course (S'04), by 9 percentage points ($p = .001$, two tailed t-test).

[7]The most compelling support for superiority of the interactive approach came from comparisons of normalized learning gains calculated from pre-test and post-test scores in the traditional and interactive classes (Table 4). [8]Normalized learning gain is defined as the actual gain divided by the possible gain, expressed as a percentage (Fagan et al., 2002). [9]A comparison of the F'03 and S'04 courses showed a significant 16% difference ($p = .001$) in average learning gains, corresponding to a 33% improvement in performance by students in the more interactive S'04 course.

6 **Read Text 1 again and identify the functions (a–d) that sentences 1–9 perform in the text. Some sentences may perform more than one function.**

a to direct readers to the table where the results can be found
b to explain the particular features of methods used
c to highlight the most important findings
d to comment on the results

Language focus

7 **Read sentences 1 and 7 in Text 1 and examples A–D below, which show how authors refer to tables in articles. Answer the questions.**

1 Which sentences and examples direct readers to a table?
2 Which sentences and examples direct readers to a table and also highlight the important findings?
3 Which tenses are used in these sentences and examples? Why?

Example A: Viability of dormant seeds was highest for wetland species (Table 2), which were also the youngest seeds.

Example B: Table 2 displays the source of support amongst older people who reported a difficulty.

Example C: The marital status of the two institutions' students differed considerably, even among the oldest graduates (Table 3).

Example D: The individual demographic and clinical data are presented in Table 1.

8 **In Text 1 underline phrases and clauses which show that the authors were comparing two different courses. Which of them use comparative forms, which superlative forms and which neither?**

9 **Fill in the gaps in the Language Support box with adjectives and adverbs from Text 1.**

Language Support: intensifying

<table>
<tr><td>We / Waters (2011) found
A comparison showed</td><td>slight
substantial
considerable
____
extreme</td><td>differences between ... and ...</td></tr>
</table>

<table>
<tr><td>Data</td><td>contrast(s/ed)

differ(s/ed)
is/are/was/were</td><td>__________
____
considerably
____
extremely</td><td>with ...

from ...
different from ...</td></tr>
</table>

Writing

10 Add phrases from Text 1 to the Language Support box.

> **Language Support: highlighting the main results**
> As Table 1 shows, there is a significant difference between …
> From the data in this table, it is clear that …
> The most striking result to emerge from the data is that …
> ______________________________
> ______________________________

11 **Work in pairs. Look at the graph from the article 'Encouraging Reflection' (see pages 65 and 80–1). Discuss the questions.**

1 What method was used to collect the data?
2 How many times did the researchers collect the data?
3 Do you think the authors are satisfied with the results? What helped you to decide?

Graph 1. Reasons for reflection

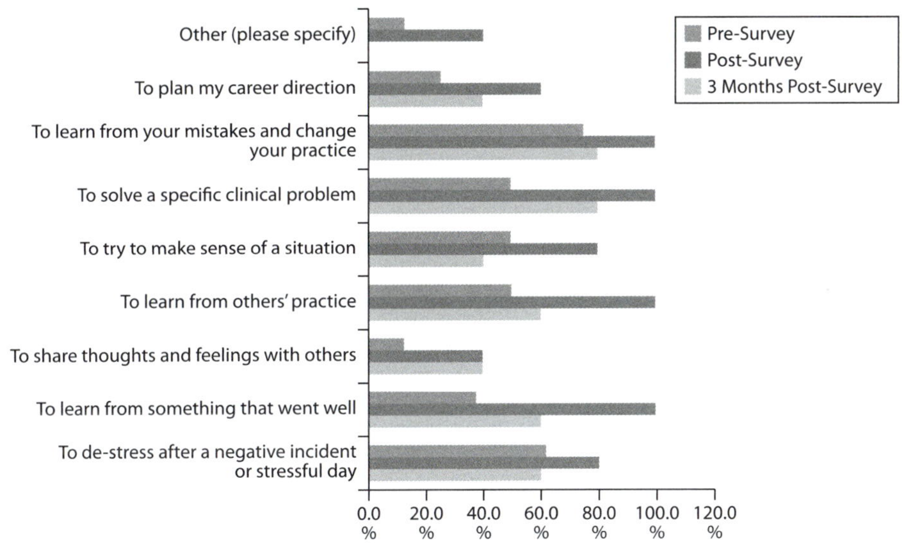

12 **Complete Text 2 with the correct form of the words in brackets. Compare your answers in Activity 11 with Text 2.**

Text 2

[1]Graph 1 displays the various scenarios in which participants [a]_______________ (*frequent*) reflect. [2]The pre-RPC (Reflective Practice Course) results indicate that the [b]_______________ (*frequent*) reason to reflect was 'to learn from your mistakes and change your practice'. [3]The post-survey results demonstrate a [c]_______________ (*considerable*) increase in all categories, with four categories receiving 100%. [4]In addition, when comparing the post- and 3 months post-results, there was a [d]_______________ (*slight*) decrease in [e]_______________ (*frequent*) at 3 months in all categories. [5]However, the overall frequency in each category at 3 months remained [f]_______________ (*great*) than at the pre-survey level. [6]These results suggest that a [g]_______________ (*positive*) shift in participants' value of reflection may occur during and after the RPC.

13 **Work in pairs. Find the sentence in Text 2 which**

1 directs readers to the visual
2 comments on the results obtained

Follow-up

14 **Read the Results section of an article from your field of study. Choose any description of the main results with reference to visuals. Identify its functions from the list below. Underline phrases which helped you to identify each element.**

- directing the reader to a table or figure
- explaining the particular features of the methods used (optional)
- highlighting the main findings
- commenting on the results (optional)

15 **Write a draft description of your research results. Exchange your draft with your partner and suggest improvements, if any. Check if your partner**

- has given key information presented in a table or figure
- has directed readers to the appropriate table or figure
- has highlighted the main results
- has written the section in a formal style
- has avoided grammar, vocabulary and spelling mistakes.

Unit 4 Coming to conclusions

By the end of this unit you will be able to
- ➡ explain your findings in the Discussion section of an article
- ➡ describe the conclusions of your study
- ➡ understand the process of submitting an article for publication
- ➡ write a covering email with an article submitted for publication

Lesson 1 The Discussion section

Lead-in

1 Work in pairs. Answer the questions.

1 Do journals in your field of study allow a separate Discussion section?
2 If not, is it combined with the Results section or the Conclusion section?
3 Which section of an article might be less objective, in your opinion?

Reading

2 Text 1 is part of the Discussion section of the article 'Being Grateful: Does it Bring Us Closer? Gratitude, Attachment and Intimacy in Romantic Relationships' (see pages 76, 82 and 91). Read it and match the highlighted words with their meanings (a–g).

a __________ – a limitation
b __________ – an average number or amount
c __________ – a measurement problem when clusters of scores are near the upper limit of the data
d __________ – a connection
e __________ – a range of numbers used as a system to measure or compare things
f __________ – an investigation aimed at proving the reliability and relevance of a procedure for a specific purpose
g __________ – points

Text 1

[1]This study investigated the association between gratitude and intimacy in romantic relationships. [2]The first hypothesis predicted a significant, positive association between gratitude and intimacy, and this hypothesis was supported; individuals who experienced more gratitude were also likely to experience more intimacy. [3]However, the association was much weaker than expected. [4]It may be that the data represent the true nature of the relationship between gratitude and intimacy, although it is also possible that measurement-related issues influenced these results. [5]As noted earlier, scores for gratitude and intimacy were highly negatively skewed resulting from largely positive responses. [6]These results may indicate that participants in this sample had a grateful outlook on life and experienced high levels of intimacy in their romantic relationships. [7]However, it is likely that such results indicate a restriction of range imposed

skewed: seeming higher or lower than they really are

by a ceiling effect. [8]It is significant that, as identified earlier, findings of other studies using the same measures (Sinclair & Dowdy, 2005) also indicate generally positive responses. [9]In particular, the validation study for the Emotional Intimacy Scale (Sinclair & Dowdy, 2005) had a significantly higher mean compared to the present study. [10]This comparison of findings may suggest that the measures of gratitude and intimacy used in this study do not identify sufficient difference between participants scoring at the high end of the scale.

3 Match elements of the Discussion section (a–f) with relevant sentences in Text 1 (1–10). Not all elements are included in Text 1.

a A reference to the *main purpose* or *hypothesis* of the study.
b A review of the most important *findings* (whether or not they support the original hypothesis, and whether they agree with the findings of other researchers).
c Possible *explanations for* or *speculations about* findings, often supported by references to relevant literature.
d *Limitations* of the study that restrict the extent to which the findings can be generalised.
e *Implications* of the study (generalisations from the results).
f *Recommendations* for future research and/or *practical.*

4 Work in pairs. Compare your answers in Activity 3.

5 Work in pairs. Answer the questions.

1 How do authors usually order the information in their discussion: from general to specific or from specific to general?
2 Are references to other publications used to support the reported findings or to indicate a gap in them?
3 What is the main difference between the Results section and the Discussion section of an article?

6 Read some phrases used to write the Discussion section and write next to them *E* for explanations, *L* for limitations and *I* for implications.

1 These data must be interpreted with caution because ...
2 One of the issues that emerges from these findings is ...
3 The findings of this study are consistent with those of Brown (2011), who found ...
4 The present study has several limitations that should be considered. First, ...
5 These findings may help us to understand ...
6 This result may be explained by the fact that ... / by a number of different factors.
7 It seems possible that these results are due to ...
8 There might also be concerns raised regarding ...
9 These results provide further support for the hypothesis that ...

Language focus

7 Sentences can have a main clause followed by a noun clause, which begins with *that*, a question word or *if/whether*. In Text 1 find sentences with a main clause and a noun clause. Complete the table with the main clause, which indicates the authors' attitude, and the noun clause, which gives the information. The first one has been done for you.

Strength	Main clause (authors' position)	+ *that*	+Noun clause (information)
	It may be	*that*	*the data represent ...*

8 Rank the expressions in the first column in Activity 7 according to the strength of the claims made by the authors. Write *S* for strong and *W* for weak.

9 Underline the hedging language (see Activity 12 on page 73) in the sentences below from the article 'Teaching More by Lecturing Less'.

1 We believe that a substantial impact could be achieved if interactive and collaborative teaching were introduced in introductory courses and continued throughout the curriculum.
2 The students in spring 2005 chose their own groups, and thus seemed to feel more loyalty to other group members than students in spring 2004, who were assigned to their groups.
3 Ability to solve problems and in-depth understanding of underlying concepts will probably be of more use to students in the long run than any particular piece of factual information.
4 It is evident that café-style classrooms would be far more conducive to active-engagement teaching.
5 Evaluation of teaching could be based on actual student learning gains as well as student course ratings.
6 Few instructors can hope to deliver more than one or two such lectures, at best, during a semester.
7 While lecturing in small doses remains a valuable teaching technique, lecturing for an entire period of 50 or 75 minutes is unlikely to be the best use of class time.

10 In Activity 9 find two sentences with a noun clause.

Writing

11 Write five sentences suitable for the Discussion section of your article. Give possible explanations for the results you described in Unit 3, Lesson 3 (see Activity 15 on page 96). Use the sentence openers in Activity 6 and hedging expressions.

12 In Text 1 find two expressions used to refer to information given previously. Add them to the list in the Language Support box. Where are they usually placed in a sentence?

> **Language Support: transition phrases**
>
> Transition phrases are used to make academic texts easier to follow. They highlight connections between different parts of a text. These expressions refer the reader to what was written earlier in the same text.
>
> As was mentioned in the Introduction, ...
> As described in the previous section, ...
> As discussed above, ...
> As explained earlier, ...
> As stated above, ...
> In addition to the above, ...
>
> ....
>
> ....

13 Revise your drafts from Activity 11 by referring to the previous sections of your article. Use the transition phrases.

14 Exchange your texts with a partner who works in your area of specialism. Read your partner's text. Suggest any possible limitations of the study. Write two or three sentences using the expressions from Activity 6.

Follow-up

15 Find two articles in your research area, one in English, one in your native language. Read the Discussion sections in both. Underline all the examples of hedging language used in these articles. Count

- the overall number of hedging expressions in every text
- the number of hedging structures used.

Lesson 2 The Conclusions section

Lead-in

1 Finish the sentence and share it with the whole class.

A conclusion is the place where ...

2 Work in pairs. Read the sentences and say which is true for you. Why?

1 I start with the Abstract and Introduction and write the Conclusions at the end.
2 I start with the Conclusions and revise them when my article is finished.
3 I start with the Results, then I write the Conclusions and revise the whole article.
4 I do it differently.

Reading

3 Read statements 1–8 about the Conclusions section of journal articles. Write *T* if the statements are true or *F* if they are false. Compare your answers in pairs.

1 This section is compulsory within the structure of the article.
2 In it the author may give recommendations for future research.
3 Focusing on the validity of findings is good practice.
4 This is the last chance to add an argument that you have forgotten to include earlier.
5 It must contain a statement about the contribution of the research findings to knowledge in the relevant field.
6 It should contain evidence to illustrate the researcher's key findings.
7 It is advisable to point out the practical applications of your study here.
8 It should give evidence to show that your findings are noteworthy.

4 Read Text 1 – the final part of the article on 'grazing' (see pages 66, 75 and 90). Which statements in Activity 3 are true of this Conclusions section?

Text 1

The principal aim of this study was to construct a new self-report measure of 'grazing' and evaluate its initial properties. Taken together, the results provided initial evidence for the favourable properties of the Grazing Questionnaire and contributed to the first operational definition of grazing that includes both unplanned, repetitive eating of small amounts of food and a sense of loss of control over eating. At the same time, it is also important to acknowledge that the homogenous nature of the present sample may limit the generalisability of our findings. Participants in the present study were mostly healthy, young, educated individuals representing high socioeconomic backgrounds. Further research concerning the prevalence of the 'grazing' pattern of eating in the wider community, in individuals with binge-eating difficulties, and in overweight and obese populations is now needed. In addition to the need for establishing the generalisability of our findings to other populations, future research may now follow on the promising results from the present study by further developing the Grazing Questionnaire and by exploring the nature, causes and effects of grazing in more detail. Adding new items based on expert or participant feedback on the content of the Grazing Questionnaire may be promising avenues for future research. Examining whether scores on the Grazing Questionnaire predict weight gain or response to treatments would be an important step in evaluating the importance of grazing in obesity and its treatment. In the meantime, our current results provide the first empirical description of a potentially important eating pattern, and the only reliable self-report measure to assess it.

high socioeconomic backgrounds: middle and upper classes

5 Read Text 1 again. Find the phrase similar in meaning to 'possible future research priorities'.

6 Work in pairs. What is the main focus of Text 1? Write out the phrases that express it.

7 Read the first part of Text 2. Which sentence signals the need for further research? Add the corresponding expression to the list in Activity 6.

Text 2

a ___*1*___ This study aimed to develop a greater understanding of the function of gratitude in romantic relationships.
b ______ Intimacy has also been identified as important in sustaining and developing satisfying relationships (Tolstedt & Stokes, 1983). This study predicted a positive association between gratitude and intimacy and, although weak, this association was demonstrated.
c ______ It proposed that experiences of gratitude expressed between partners would lead to experiences of intimacy.
d ______ Although this effect was not evident in the findings of this study, a careful analysis of the data suggest the presence of ceiling effects and therefore these should be regarded as inconclusive, rather than negative findings.
e ______ In addition, this study predicted that attachment would moderate the association between gratitude and intimacy.

Language focus

8 **Put the sentences in Text 2 (a–e) in the order you think the authors originally wrote them. What language helps you to do this?**

9 **Choose the correct options to create the second part of Text 2.**

[1]*This / That* study identifies a number of gaps [2]*in / of* current understandings [3]*with / of* gratitude and intimacy. [4]*That / It* also highlights the need [5]*to / for* further research [6]*into / to* the function of gratitude and intimacy [7]*on / in* romantic relationships. [8]*In / For* particular, it recommends the investigation [9]*of / about* specific experiences [10]*in / of* gratitude and intimacy [11]*to / for* both partners. [12]*So / Such* future investigations have the potential to develop more comprehensive understandings [13]*in / of* the function of gratitude [14]*across / in* romantic relationships. [15]*These / Any* promising avenues [16]*to / for* further research may also provide a foundation [17]*for / of* developing therapeutic interventions for couples [18]*which / who* wish [19]*that / to* improve [20]*their / theirs* relationships.

Writing and Speaking

10 **Develop your Discussion section. Write 4–5 sentences describing the limitations of your research and the need for further study.**

11 **Exchange your drafts. Read your partner's text and make a list of questions about**

- his/her main purpose or hypothesis
- the most important findings
- their interpretation of the results
- the limitations of their study
- the recommendations for future research
- the practical applications of their study.

12 **Work in pairs. Ask and answer the questions in Activity 11.**

Follow-up

13 Revise the draft of the abstract you produced in Unit 1, Lesson 3 (see Activity 12 on page 68). Check if you have

- included the aim, background, methods, results and conclusions
- focused on the most important ideas
- used language appropriately
- written your text logically
- avoided spelling, vocabulary and grammar mistakes.

Lesson 3 The article submission process

Lead-in

1 Work in groups. Discuss the questions.

1 You have written an article for publication. How long does it usually take to get it published?
2 What are the steps towards this goal? Present your ideas in a diagram or a flow chart.

Listening

2 26 Listen to a conference presenter speaking on the topic of getting published. Write *T* if the statements below are true or *F* if they are false.

1 The presenter recommends writing to the editor before submitting an article.
2 He says that the covering letter should contain information about the authors of the article.
3 All the authors of the article should see the final version of their text before it is submitted.
4 The presenter says that articles often get rejected because of the poor quality of the language.
5 He recommends sending the paper to another journal if it is rejected after the peer review.
6 If the paper is accepted, the journal staff works on it and then puts it online or prints it.

Language focus

3 26 List the groups of people who are involved in the process of writing and publication. Does the presenter mention all of them? Listen again and check your answers.

4 Read the words and phrases in the box and find the odd one out.

editing and proof-reading	peer review	acceptance (with revisions)			
submission	resubmitting	publishing	complaining	rejection	revisions

5 Fill in the flow chart with the appropriate words from Activity 4 in the correct order.

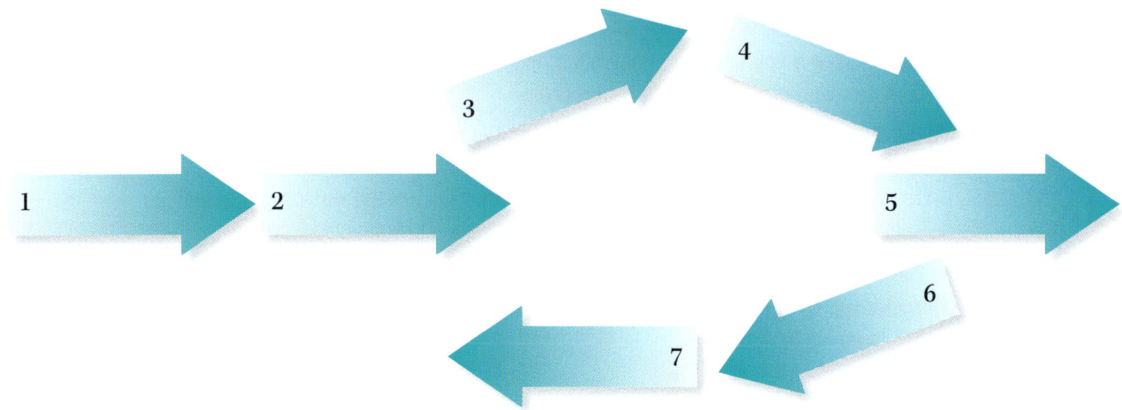

Reading

6 Read Texts 1 and 2 quickly. Say at which stage of the submission process each of them was written. Explain your answers.

Text 1

To: fin-journal@gmail.com

Subject: ____________

Dear Dr Liffits,

Please find attached a manuscript entitled 'Combined classifiers in bankruptcy prediction for manufacturing companies' by Elena Fodor, Samuel Dovzen and myself. The authors have read and approved the final version submitted here.

There has been a great deal of research in the field of bankruptcy forecasting. Our research distinguishes itself from previous publications in the following respects.

1. We use a wide range of financial indicators, including those considered in classical and modern literature and those recommended by different countries' legislative practices.
2. We employ combinations of different modern techniques to choose appropriate financial indicators and achieve higher forecasting efficiency.
3. We use a large dataset of manufacturing companies for the period 2007–2011.

We would be very grateful if you would consider the manuscript for publication in the *International Financial Review*.

Yours sincerely,
Eugene Gilko

Corresponding author: Eugene Gilko

34 Anbor Str., Nemburg, Levonia

Text 2

To: gardot@mail.com

Subject: ____________

Dear Prof. Gardot,

First of all, we [1] are thanking you and the anonymous reviewer for the valuable feedback and the opportunity to resubmit our paper to your journal.

We have made the changes you and the reviewer suggested. We [2] sent a revised manuscript entitled 'External spillover effects for countries in transition: a multivariate approach' by Tim Anderson and Elena Fodor. Both authors [3] read and approved the final revised version submitted here. In the revised manuscript the corrections [4] we have made are shown in bold type.

We [5] are providing answers to the reviewer's comments.

We believe the paper is now acceptable for publication and [6] look forward to your response to the changes we have made.

Yours sincerely,
Elena Fodor

Corresponding author: Elena Fodor

35 Shelley Road, Cambridge CB27 4TT 44 (0)1223 44670

External spillover: an effect that results from a problem spreading

7 In Text 2 find four mistakes in the highlighted verb forms. Correct them.

Speaking

8 Work in pairs. Read Texts 1 and 2 again and follow the steps below.

1 Fill in the subject lines. Compare your versions with another pair.
2 Say which advice from the presenter's talk the authors follow in their covering emails.

9 ⦿26 Read the Language Support box. Listen again to Track 26 and say which of these ways of adding emphasis are used by the presenter.

> **Language Support: adding emphasis**
> ***It … that/who*** sentences, e.g. *It is the author who is responsible for properly formatting the manuscript.*
> ***What … is*** clauses, e.g. *What many authors fail to take into account is the relevance of their material to the type of journal in which they want to publish.*
> The auxiliary verb ***do*** before the main verb in statements and imperatives, e.g. *You **do need** to carefully edit your text before sending it to the journal.*
> *Do take the reviewers' comments seriously.*

10 Work in pairs. Talk to your partner about times when you have had problems with publishing an article (e.g. with guidelines, deadlines, reviews, formatting, proof-reading). Ask your partner to give you advice on how to avoid these situations. Use the structures in the Language Support box to add emphasis to your conversation.

A: *Two years ago I sent an article about teaching biology to a journal but they rejected it. They said they don't publish articles on methodology.*

B: *You do need to check beforehand if the journal accepts papers related to the subject of your article.*

Writing

11 Write a draft of a covering email for submission of your paper on research you have done. Use Text 1 as a model.

12 Work in pairs. Exchange emails and check your partner's text. Make comments if necessary.

Follow-up

13 Work in groups. Follow the steps below.

1 Choose a journal in your native language which publishes articles in your field of research. Read its guidelines for authors. Look through the structure, format and style of its articles.
2 Make a group presentation on how to get published in this journal.
3 As a whole class, discuss the pros and cons of publishing nationally or internationally.

Module wrapping-up

1 You have finished Module 2. Congratulations! Reflect on the module and evaluate your progress. Finalise your article. Read the statements in the table below and tick them if you agree with them.

Module 2	
Checklist for preparing an article for publication	
My article is suitable for publication in the journal I have chosen.	
The contribution is new and significant.	
The organisation of the article is acceptable.	
There are no errors or faults of logic.	
The title is clear, concise and effective.	
Suggested keywords are appropriate.	
My abstract is written to the required standard. It is clear and short.	
The methods are sound and they are described clearly.	
My illustrations and tables (if required) are properly prepared and accurately referred to.	
The conclusions are supported by sufficient evidence.	
All relevant references are cited and formatted correctly.	
The length of my article is satisfactory.	

2 What do you need to improve further? Set yourself some goals for further development. Use the SMART principle: goals should be Specific, Measurable, Achievable, Realistic, Time-bound.

3 Share your responses to the module with the whole class.

Module 3

Teaching and learning in English

In this module you will:

- write a syllabus for the subject you teach in English
- discuss and practise up-to-date approaches and technologies in teaching your subject in English

Unit 1 Teaching around the globe

By the end of this unit you will be able to

- describe current trends in higher education in your country
- report on recent changes in your educational institution
- discuss the use of technology in teaching your subject
- write your academic profile or the academic profile of a colleague

Lesson 1 Facing the changes

Lead-in

1 Work in pairs. At the end of this lesson you are going to report on recent changes in your institution. Discuss the questions.

- What changes have taken place in the last five years in your educational institution?
- Which changes have been positive? Why?
- Which changes have been less positive? Why?

Reading

2 Text 1 summarises predictions about the development of higher education. Read Part 1 quickly and complete the sentence below.

The text is written from a

a Chinese perspective.
b British perspective.
c European perspective.
d student perspective.

Text 1 Part 1

The British Council projects that the [1] ________________ for higher education worldwide will continue to grow to 2020 but at a lower rate than in the last two decades.

The number of [2] ________________ will grow significantly by 2020, although at a slower pace than in previous years. Reasons for this slowdown include stagnant demand in the developed world, a sharp decrease in the size of the 18–24 age cohort in key countries such as China, growing supply in the BRIC (Brazil-Russia-India-China) countries and further expansion of TNE (transnational education) and [3] ________________ .

The British Council expects that the largest numbers of mobile students in 2020 will be from China, India, South Korea, Germany, Turkey, Malaysia, Nigeria, Kazakhstan and France.

Europe will continue to be the preferred [4] ________________ for international students worldwide by 2020. The main English-speaking exporting countries along with Germany, France and Japan will [5] ________________ their leading positions by 2020. China will emerge, perhaps not by 2020, as a powerhouse in higher education that will set the rules for doing business there.

In several European countries, including Germany and France, governments aim to [6]________________ higher education systems and to provide more courses in English in order to attract more [7]________________ .

The demand for UK [8]________________ abroad will hold up in the foreseeable future, even as the UK share of the global student market will continue to decrease. UK qualifications are perceived to be among the best in the world: that has not changed.

The way students [9]________________ higher education is changing. By 2020, the traditional and well-established route followed by a full-time, residential, three-year [10]________________ will be only one pathway among many.

3 Read Part 1 of Text 1 again and complete it with the words in the box.

enter qualifications demand degree distance education maintain mobile students international students destination internationalise

4 Read Part 1 again and answer the questions.

1 What do the abbreviations *TNE* and *BRIC* stand for?
2 In what connection are these countries/areas mentioned?
BRIC Europe China Germany France

5 Read Part 2 of Text 1. Write *T* if the statements below are true, *F* if they are false or *NS* if it is not stated.

1 MOOCs will result in a decrease in student mobility.
2 A 'badge' course doesn't allow students to earn credits toward a degree.
3 Traditional classes will be fully replaced by online learning.
4 The administration of exams and exchange of coursework over the internet will become the norm.
5 Workers with IT skills will continue to be in demand.
6 Partnerships are a form of higher education internationalisation.

Text 1 Part 2

Developments in online technology are seen as already having an impact on pedagogy, internationalisation strategies, and on how universities are run as businesses. Knowledge will increasingly be seen as a global public good through expanded access to open educational resources.

Growth in TNE will accelerate to meet growing demand. TNE refers to arrangements by which students are taught in their own or third countries; it includes online and distance learning, validation and franchising, and international branch campuses.

validation: official approval

franchising: the right to sell

Another factor to consider is the impact of MOOCs (Massive Open Online Courses) on higher education. MOOCs are unlikely to have a negative impact on either TNE or international student mobility. Students will choose courses from different institutions and receive credit toward a degree or non-degree certificate or 'badge'. However, students prefer blended to 100% online learning.

Technological innovation will affect the types of skills sought by employers. If predictions about the automation of manufacturing and the importance of big data prove to be correct, employers will increasingly look for workers with skills in software engineering, 3D design, coding and data analysis.

The internationalisation of HE includes a wide range of activities: exchanges of staff and students, TNE, internationalising the curriculum at home, and the formation of highly integrated forms of partnerships. These forms include joint academic posts, offer joint courses, and will begin to offer integrated degree programmes, rather than joint or dual degrees. Partnerships with business and industry at the international level will provide new funding flows and employability opportunities.

In higher education, changes in job structures should follow the online revolution. Junior lecturers may be gradually replaced by mentors, scattered around the world and with only a loose connection with their employers; more senior academics might have multiple contracts with several higher education institutions. The model of the academic who spends her or his entire academic career in one or two institutions is already a peculiarity and will disappear, perhaps not by 2020, but soon enough.

The influence of rankings is the clearest demonstration of the increasingly competitive nature of higher education. A common view of international rankings is that they cannot measure all of the things that universities are good at. They tell only partial and biased stories about universities: that they are commercially driven, that there is no consensus on an ideal university, but that they 'are here to stay'. Governments refer to international rankings for policy-making in education.

mentor: someone who gives another person help and advice over a period of time

Language focus

6 **Read Parts 1 and 2 of Text 1 again. Find phrases that describe positive changes, negative changes or no change. Add them to the Language Support box.**

> **Language Support: describing trends**
>
> ... is becoming (increasingly) popular.
> ... are expected to increase (to just 30%)
> ... have risen (so) (dramatically) (recently)
>
> *continue to grow* ______________________
>
> ______________________
>
> ______________________
>
> ______________________
>
> ... which has further reduced (to ...)
>
> *at a lower rate than ...* ______________________
>
> ______________________
>
> ______________________
>
> ______________________
>
> ______________________
>
> remained (almost) the same (as ...)
>
> *continue to be* ______________________

7 **To prepare for your report on recent changes in your institution, read Part 2 of Text 1 again and write out the examples of: types of learning, skills in demand and forms of partnership that are relevant to your institution.**

8 **Work in groups. Describe three trends in higher education in your country, using phrases from Activities 6 and 7.**

9 **Correct the mistakes in the use of prepositions in the sentences.**

1 He referred in a history book to find out the dates of the French Revolution.
2 They followed about her academic progress closely.
3 These changes seem to me to be happening in too fast a pace.
4 These measures are intended to soften the impact of the tax reform in people.
5 New technologies continue to affect on how we live.

Listening

10 27 **Listen to a teacher describing recent changes in her department. Answer the questions.**

1 What changes does the speaker mention?
2 What is the main aim of these changes?

11 27 **Listen again and fill in the gaps in Text 2.**

Text 2

I'd like to report on the changes that have taken place in the department I work for.

Over the last few years the department has introduced some [1] ______________ in order to meet a [2] ______________ for the internationalisation of higher education. For example, the department is seeking more partnerships with European universities. The [3] ______________ with French, Finnish and Bulgarian universities has resulted in [4] ______________ programmes in International Business and International Tourism. Currently, we are negotiating a joint master's degree course in International Business and Governance with four Italian universities. Another change worth mentioning is an [5] ______________ number of online courses.

We really think that all this will [6] ______________ student mobility and attract more [7] ______________ students. As a [8] ______________ to this challenging aim, we have already started offering some courses in English. About 20 foreign students are [9] ______________ in the European Studies programme. However, not all lecturers are competent enough in English to teach their [10] ______________ to international students. That is why there is a need to [11] ______________ academics' English language skills.

In conclusion, we think the changes that [12] ______________ may enhance the university's standing in international rankings.

12 Add phrases from Text 2 to the Language Support box. You will need them to structure your own report.

Language Support: structuring a report

1 Introduction
This is my report on ...
I'd like to describe/talk about ...
After studying ..., it was found that ...
____

2 Providing evidence
With regard to ...
In support of ...
____
____

3 Prediction
I believe that ...
It is predicted that ...
____

4 Conclusion
For the reasons given above, ...
To sum up, ...
____

Follow-up

13 Prepare a 1–2 minute report on the changes that have taken place in your department / educational institution over the last five years. Search for the information, if necessary. You may want to answer the following questions.

1 Has the number of international students changed over the last few years? What countries do they come from?
2 What new programmes (e.g. bachelor's, master's, courses in English) and forms of learning does your university offer to students?
3 What forms of partnership is your department/university involved in?

Use the language in the Language Support boxes.

14 Work in groups. Present your report to your colleagues and listen to theirs. Ask and answer questions.

Lesson 2 The impact of technology

Lead-in

1 **Work in groups. Read two opinions about the impact of technology on education. Discuss which one you support and why.**

A

> Technology has created a lack of depth in learning; students who are bombarded by technological inputs might be more inclined to skim the surface information on many topics without truly getting an in-depth understanding of any of them.

B

> We now have the technological tools to disseminate knowledge to students across the globe. No longer limited by geography, a student can learn from some of the best and brightest sources in the world, no matter where they are, as long as there is an internet connection available.

Listening

2 28 **Listen to a teacher talking about technology and education. Is she happy about how technology is used in education? Why? / Why not?**

3 28 **Listen again and answer the questions.**

1 What does she see as the conflict between formal education and technology?
2 How can teachers benefit from using technology?
3 How can students benefit from using technology?

4 **Work in groups. Discuss the questions.**

1 To what extent do the same tensions exist in your working context?
2 How has your job as a teacher changed over the last five years?

Reading

5 **Read Text 1 on the next page about new pedagogical models brought in by advances in technology. Which of the paragraphs (A–C) discusses**

1 research activities using mobile devices
2 self-directed learning
3 an example of a discipline in which technology can effectively be used
4 learning from other people
5 a mix of digital opportunities and natural surroundings
6 activities tailored for individual interests
7 a risk of using technology in learning

Text 1

Innovating Pedagogy 2013

The innovations described in this report are not technologies looking for an application in formal education. They are new ways of teaching, learning and assessment. If they are to succeed, they need to complement formal education, rather than trying to replace it.

A Crowd learning: Crowd learning describes the process of learning [1]__________ the expertise and opinions of others, shared [2]__________ online social spaces, websites, and activities. Such learning is often informal and spontaneous, and may not be recognised [3]__________ the participants as a learning activity. In this model virtually anybody can be a teacher or source of knowledge, learning occurs flexibly and sporadically, can be driven [4]__________ chance or specific goals, and always has direct contextual relevance [5]__________ the learner. It places responsibility [6]__________ individual learners to find a path through sources of knowledge and to manage the objectives of their learning. Crowd learning encourages people to be active [7]__________ setting personal objectives, seeking resources, and recording achievements. It can also develop the skills needed [8]__________ lifelong learning, such as self-motivation and reflection [9]____ performance. The challenge is to provide learners [10]__________ ways to manage their learning and offer valuable contributions [11]__________ others.

B Seamless learning: Seamless learning (connecting learning experiences across the contexts of location, time, device and social setting) is [1]__________ (*move*) from research to mainstream adoption. Mobile technologies enable learners of all ages to operate across contexts, for example schools allowing students to bring their own devices. Pedagogy is [2]__________ (*emerge*), [3]__________ (*base*) on learners [4]__________ (*start*) an investigation in class, then [5]__________ (*collect*) data at home or outdoors, [6]__________ (*construct*) new knowledge with assistance from the software, and [7]__________ (*share*) findings in the classroom. There is also a broader notion of seamless learning [8]__________ (*arise*) from [9]__________ (*connect*) experience. Our activities online are increasingly [10]__________ (*match*) to our interests: search pages order responses based on previous queries; websites recommend content [11]__________ (*relate*) to our past viewing. The benefits are that personally relevant information may be ready to hand, but the danger is that we may come to believe that our views, preferences and connections are not just the most relevant, but all there is.

queries: questions

C Geo-learning: Sensors built into mobile devices, such as smartphones and tablets, can determine a user's location and provide context-aware educational resources in the surrounding environment. [1]*These / Those* can enable both formal and informal learning within physical 'real-world' settings. [2]*They / It* may also enhance and frame the subject matter being studied. For example, learning about an historical event could be situated in the place where [3]*that/those* event occurred, giving a rich sensory experience of being in the scene. Fieldwork activities have long encompassed 'geo-learning' as a way of providing information [4]*that / what* exploits the surroundings and landscape. Geo-learning is not new; however technologies sensitive to location, or embedded in objects near the learner, now allow greater mixing of digital information with the physical world, to produce 'blended spaces'. We need to consider carefully [5]*how / what* we employ [6]*these / those* opportunities for learning. Current theories are somewhat limited, but several approaches, including research into learning spaces, provide ways to model the richness of [7]*these / those* environments and our interactions within them.

encompassed: included
embedded: fixed firmly

Language focus

6 **Read Paragraph A of Text 1 again. Fill in the gaps with the prepositions in the box.**

with	from	to	to	through	by	by	in	on	on	for

7 **Read the Language Support box. Then complete Paragraph B in Text 1 with the correct form of the verbs given in brackets.**

Language Support: present and past participles

The present participle (verb+*ing*) is used for continuous tenses, e.g. *He is lecturing in Room 253.*
The past participle (verb+*ed*) is used with perfect tenses and the passive, e.g. *The schedule has been changed.*
Both participles are also used in short phrases that function as clauses. Compare these examples:
Working alone, he managed to complete the whole report. (The participle refers to the subject of the clause that follows.)
The article published last month completely changed the approach to the problem. (The past participle here stands for a relative clause: *The article which was published* ...)

8 **Choose the right word in Paragraph C of Text 1 from each pair in italics.**

9 **Complete these verb + noun collocations from Text 1. Check them in the text. In some cases, more than one option is possible.**

1 ______________ responsibility on somebody to do something
2 ______________ personal objectives
3 ______________ on performance
4 manage ______________
5 ______________ the subject matter
6 employ ______________
7 ______________ learning

10 **Write questions for the following answers. Use phrases from Activity 9. The underlined words in the answers will help you to choose the phrases. The first one has been done for you.**

1 Hearing some personal stories made the subject matter more alive and relevant to the students.
What enhanced the subject matter for the students?
2 Oh yes, he is absolutely independent. He doesn't need a teacher to help him learn.
____
3 Well, I've created a plan of further activities after thinking about the results.
____
4 No, it was Prof. Bobkov who was put in charge of the experimental work.
____
5 I decided that my goal was to get an article published by the end of the course.
____

11 **Read Text 1 again and fill in the table with short notes. Some have been added for you.**

Learning model	Main concept	Learning activities	Features	Problems and challenges
Crowd learning	• *Learning from others*			
Seamless learning			• *Connected learning experiences* • *Personally relevant*	
Geo-learning		• *Doing fieldwork* • *Mixing digital information with the physical world*		

12 **Work in groups. Discuss the questions, using your notes in Activity 11.**

1 What are the advantages of each pedagogical model?
2 What limitations do these models have?
3 Could any of the models be applied to the teaching of your own subject?

13 **Work in groups. Prepare for a discussion about how the use of technology influences the teaching of your subject. Follow the steps below.**

1 Think of questions you would like to discuss. For example:
What are the advantages and disadvantages of using technology to teach your subject?
2 Agree on the three most important questions for the discussion.
3 Read these 'Ground Rules' for discussion. Do you agree with them? Are there any others you want to add?
   - Use only English.
   - Everyone should contribute.
   - Listen carefully to what other people say and respond.
   - Don't interrupt the speaker until he/she has finished.
   - Control your voice and behaviour.
   - Stick to the time limit.

4 Choose a discussion leader. This person's job is to start the discussion by asking the discussion questions, and to make sure everyone has a turn speaking. Discussion leaders should read the notes 'Leading a discussion' on page 166.

14 **Prepare what you are going to say in two minutes about the use of technology in your subject, based on the questions you agreed on in Activity 13. Think of examples of using technology. Note down your ideas.**

15 **Work in the same groups as in Activity 13 and discuss the questions you agreed on. Use what you prepared in Activity 14. Discussion leaders will start the discussion and make notes.**

Follow-up

16 **Discussion leaders summarise the points the groups made and report back to the whole class.**

Lesson 3 Your academic profile

Lead-in

1 Read the list of requirements that might be necessary for an international visiting professor. Rank them from the most important (1) to the least important (10).

- knowledge of a foreign language
- publications in the field of study
- experience in teaching
- previous international projects
- a good CV
- a strong track record in research
- awareness of cultural differences
- the ability to be open to other cultures
- good communication and presentation skills
- advanced technological skills

2 Work in groups. Discuss your ranking of requirements in Activity 1.

Listening

3 ⊙29 Listen to the first part of a radio programme about using technology in education and answer the questions,

1 How did the speaker know Professor Nellie Deustch?
2 How did she ask her for an interview?
3 What does the speaker thank her for?

4 ⊙30 Listen to Professor Deutsch's answers and write down the five questions you think she was asked.

5 ⊙30 Listen again and fill in the gaps with the phrases that help to paraphrase or expand on each idea.

1 I was able to use technology to reach each one of my students outside the classroom. ____________, I connected with them from home ...
2 I started connecting my students with other teachers around the world, and that made it more exciting. ____________, I took my students out of the classroom.
3 I was thinking about how I was going to reach my students and they were going to reach each other. ____________, it became a socially engaging endeavour.
4 I was experimenting and I found the methods as a result. ____________, I wasn't learning from the literature that was available, I was doing what I felt was intuitively right.

6 ⊙31 Listen to the questions and compare them with those you have written in Activity 4. How would you answer the same five questions?

7 Work in groups. Discuss the questions below.

1 Would you like to be recognised internationally?
2 What can be done to promote your research/courses, etc.?

Reading

8 Read Texts 1 and 2 quickly and answer the questions. Ignore any specialist terminology.

1 What are these texts intended for?
2 Where might they have been published?

Text 1

Dr. Kirill V. Larin

Dr. Kirill V. Larin is an Associate Professor of Biomedical Engineering at the University of Houston. He also holds joint appointments at the Departments of Mechanical Engineering and Electrical and Computer Engineering at the University of Houston and Department of Optics and Biophysics at Saratov State University (SSU) in Russia.

Larin received his first M.Sc. in Laser Physics and Mathematics from the SSU (1995), his second M.Sc. in Cellular Physiology and Molecular Biophysics (2001) and Ph.D. in Biomedical Engineering from the University of Texas Medical Branch in Galveston (2002). His research contributions are in Biomedical Optics and Biophotonics and the development and application of various optical methods for the noninvasive and nondestructive imaging and diagnostics of tissues and cells.

Larin has authored more than 70 peer-reviewed journal and conference publications and chapters in several textbooks on Biomedical Optics. He is a member of the General Program Committee for the annual International Meeting on Optics, Laser Physics and Biophysics and currently a member of the Optical Society of America, American Society for Lasers in Medicine and Biology, and SPIE. His contribution to the field of optics was recognized by his nomination for the Russian Presidential Award. He has also received the Wallace Coulter Young Investigator Translation Award, the Office of Naval Research the Young Investigator Award, the Outstanding Young Investigator Award from the Houston Society for Engineers in Medicine and Biology, and the Herbert Allen Award from American Society for Mechanical Engineers.

Larin currently serves as an Instructor for short courses on Tissue Optics for the Optical Society of America.

Text 2

Dr. Peter Janiszewski

Dr. Peter Janiszewski is a medical writer and editor, published researcher, science blogger and an advocate of new media in scientific knowledge translation.

As a medical writer with an established record of working with international clients in Asia, Europe and North America, Peter produces accurate, creative, and engaging content in the form of peer-reviewed manuscripts, reviews, clinical reports, abstracts, book chapters, grant proposals, educational content, newsletters, slide decks, posters, websites, blogs, and online social media.

As a researcher, Peter has published numerous studies, reviews and commentaries in prestigious peer-reviewed medical journals on topics related to exercise, diet, obesity, diabetes, cardiovascular disease, oncology, and others. He has also presented his research at various international scientific conferences and acts as a peer-reviewer for various medical journals.

To aid in the dissemination of scientific knowledge, Peter also contributes articles for the popular press, health newsletters, and has appeared in national newspapers and radio. He blogs at Obesity Panacea and Science of Blogging and is the past Health/Clinical Research Editor for ResearchBlogging.org.

9 **Read Texts 1 and 2 again and answer the questions.**

1 What do these two people have in common?
2 What differences can you find in their professional and academic activities?

10 **Work in groups. Share the ideas you had in Activity 9. Use phrases from the Language Support box 'comparison and contrast' on page 38 and the ones below.**

They are both … / They have both published / They both work …

Dr Larin is …, whereas Dr Janiszewski is …

Language focus

11 **Work in pairs. Answer the questions.**

1 Three different verb tenses are used in Text 1. What are they? Complete the sentences with their names.
   a The ______________ tells us about an action or state in the past.
   b The ______________ tells us about an action or state in the present.
   c The ______________ tells us about an action or state that began in the past and is connected to the present.
2 In Text 2, what is the connection between the first sentence and the three paragraphs that follow?
3 Why are these biographies written in the third person rather than the first person?

12 Read Text 3. What makes it different from Texts 1 and 2? What verb tense is used in this text? Why?

Text 3

Lev Vygotsky

Lev Vygotsky was born in Orsha, a city in the western region of the Russian Empire. He graduated from Moscow State University with a degree in law in 1917. He studied a range of topics there, including sociology, linguistics, psychology and philosophy. However, his formal work in psychology did not begin until 1924 when he attended the Institute of Psychology in Moscow and began collaborating with Alexei Leontiev and Alexander Luria.

Lev Vygotsky was a prolific writer: he published six books on psychology topics over a ten-year period. His interests were quite diverse, but often centred on topics of child development and education. He also explored such topics as the psychology of art and language development.

13 Find phrases in Texts 1, 2 and 3 that you can use to give information about the topics below and add them to the list.

- degrees: *to receive an MSc in … from*
- positions: *to serve as*
- research area: *(his) contribution to the field of*
- publications: *to contribute articles for*
- awards: *to receive an award from*

14 Read the Language Support box. Add phrases to those you have written in Activity 13.

Language Support: writing a professional/academic biography

… is a well-known researcher on issues relating to …
In his/her capacity as head of …
… has written a number of articles/books covering the significant issues in …
… has researched and published widely on …
… is known for his/her wide experience in …
… is/was in charge of research projects on …
… has taught …

Follow-up

15 **Write a short professional biography (60–150 words), using the language presented in this lesson. Choose one of the options below.**

- Interview a colleague and write his/her biography.
- Write your own biography.

16 **Bring your biographies to class. Read the biography of one of your classmates and give feedback. Tick the criteria given in the checklist below.**

Checklist for a professional biography	
Overall impression	
Does the text describe the person positively?	
Does it present information clearly and concisely?	
Is it logically organised?	
Content	
Does the text contain the information about	
• positions?	
• degrees?	
• fields of interest?	
• publications?	
• membership of professional bodies?	
Language	
Does the author use the present perfect, past simple and present simple appropriately?	
Are capitals used for names, organisations, courses, etc.?	

Unit 2 Designing a syllabus in English

By the end of this unit you will be able to

- identify the sections of a syllabus
- write a draft syllabus, including clear learning outcomes, for a course you teach
- write a section about assessment in the syllabus for a course you teach

Lesson 1 What is a syllabus?

Lead-in

1 Work in groups. Discuss the questions.

1 Do you have a syllabus for your subject?
2 Who designed it?
3 How often do you refer to the syllabus?

2 Match words 1–3 with definitions a–c.

1 syllabus	a a plan of activities to be done
2 curriculum	b a plan showing the topics or books to be studied in a particular course
3 programme of work	c a document listing the group of subjects studied in an educational institution

Listening

3 32 Listen to the first part of a lecture on course design and answer the questions.

1 Where does the word *syllabus* come from?
2 What are its plural forms?

4 32 Listen again and complete the definition of the word *syllabus*.

A syllabus is a brief ______ or ______ of the ______ covered in an ______.

5 Work in groups. Make a list of the functions a syllabus has.

to inform students of the aims of the course

6 33 Listen to the second part of the lecture. What functions of a syllabus does the speaker mention? Compare them with the functions you listed in Activity 4.

7 33 Listen again and answer the questions.

1 How does the speaker signal the introduction of each function?
2 Is the speaker's style of presentation formal or informal? How do you know?
3 How does the speaker involve the audience?

Reading

8 Match words 1–6 with definitions a–f.

1 assignment
2 attendance
3 grading
4 outcome
5 outline
6 aim

a a description of the main facts about something, for example, a new plan or idea
b a result that you have achieved
c giving a mark to a student's piece of work
d a piece of work given to students as part of their studies
e presence at a conference, class or similar event
f the purpose of doing something

9 Complete the sentences using words 1–6 from Activity 8.

1 The seminar ______________ may be detailed or not, depending on your expectations of students' background knowledge.
2 Explain the ______________ scale, indicating the weight of each component, such as homework, papers, exams or reports.
3 Explain in detail the policy concerning class ______________ .
4 Learning ______________ describe what students will be able to do or will know when they have completed a course.
5 Briefly describe the nature and format of the coursework ______________ .
6 The ______________ of the course is to provide an overview of some of the fundamental principles behind nanotechnology and nanomaterial.

10 Generally, a syllabus contains a number of sections. Match extracts A–G from the syllabus sections of two courses with the corresponding names of sections 1–10. Three sections do not have matching extracts.

1 Course title
2 Contact details of the tutor
3 Course description
4 Course aims
5 Student learning outcomes
6 Outline of content
7 Assignments
8 Attendance policy
9 Grading scale
10 Required reading

A

☐

Oral communication	20%
3 Papers	60%
Final project on food ethics	20%

☐ There are 3 tests and a project. In addition, each term will have a final exam. The final mark is the average of the final marks for term 1 and term 2.

B

☐ It is important that students participate in, and engage fully with all scheduled activities such as lectures, workshops and seminars. Attendance is therefore regarded as essential.

☐ Attendance at **all** lectures is **required**. Lab calculations are necessary for the final project.

C

☐ The course is designed to improve students' ability to:
– identify moral and political issues and interpret arguments relevant to food choices and policies;
– gather and evaluate information relevant to these issues.

☐ The purpose of the course is to provide students with an introduction to quantitative techniques and their applications in the context of international and business problems.

D

☐ Session 1: Introduction

Sessions 2–6: Overview of Issues and Challenges

☐ Weeks 1&2: Matrices

Weeks 3&4: Introduction to linear programming

E

☐ This course introduces students to quantitative techniques and their applications in the context of international and business problems. In addition, the course is designed to enable students to study the principles of constructing econometric and non-econometric models and how these models can be used in various practical contexts. Relevant research outcomes utilising these techniques would be highlighted.

☐ This course explores the values (aesthetic, moral, cultural, religious, prudential, political) expressed in the choices of food people eat. It analyses the decisions individuals make about what to eat, how society should manage food production and consumption collectively, and how reflection on food choices might help resolve conflicts between different values.

F

☐ Lectures: 2 sessions a week, each session 1 hour

Reading, discussing and writing about the assigned readings are the central activities of this class. There is a reading assignment for each lecture. Some are quite difficult and demand careful study.

☐ Students will have a two-hour session each week. In some weeks, this takes the form of a one-hour lecture and a one-hour tutorial/laboratory session or tutorial presentation on using statistical packages. The assigned lab tasks will lead to a final course project.

G

☐	By the end of this course, students will be able to: – interpret and analyse information in numerical form – make effective use of statistical and other packages
☐	By the end of the course students will have demonstrated their ability to: – evaluate information relevant to the issues of food choices and policies – utilise normative frameworks for making moral decisions with regard to food choices and policies.

11 **Work in pairs. The extracts in Activity 10 are taken from two different syllabuses. Write 1 or 2 in the boxes in each extract to show which syllabus each comes from:**

1 Statistics and Research Methods
2 The Ethics of Food Choice

What clues helped you to decide?

Language focus

12 **Read the Language Support box. Change the phrases with *of* or *on* below into two or more nouns together. The first one has been done for you.**

1 the design of engines of aircraft *aircraft engine design*
2 an operation on cataracts ______
3 erosion of the land ______
4 the features of the product ______
5 the department of management and finance ______
6 the results of the research ______
7 a list of references ______
8 the policy of the university ______
9 a block of offices ______
10 a leader of a team ______

Language Support: two nouns together

Very often two nouns can be used together. The first noun usually tells us what kind of thing the second noun is, e.g. *a computer virus* is a kind of virus. The first noun is always singular, e.g. *a shoe shop* (a shop of shoes), *a document folder* (a folder for documents).

The rules for article use apply to two nouns together too: *a* for the first mention of a countable noun phrase, the for a specific noun phrase, and 'zero' article for a general, uncountable noun phrase or a plural noun phrase.

13 **Read the course titles. What do you notice about the language and the use of articles in them?**

- Financial Engineering and Risk Management (Part 1)
- Applications in Engineering Mechanics
- E-learning and Digital Cultures
- Data Management for Clinical Research
- Introduction to Environmental Law and Policy
- Foundations for Virtual Instruction
- Game Theory

14 **Write the English title(s) of a course or courses you teach.**

Follow-up

15 **On the internet, search for a course syllabus similar to one you teach. Follow the steps below.**

1 Compare the sections in the syllabus you have found with the examples in this lesson.
2 In the description of the syllabus, choose phrases that can help you write your own syllabus.

16 **Work in pairs. Discuss the questions.**

1 What kind of syllabus have you found? Which university offers this course?
2 Is the structure of the syllabus you have found similar to the two presented in this lesson? If not, what are the differences?
3 Is the structure of the syllabus different from the requirements in your university? If yes, what are the differences?

17 **Work in pairs. Exchange the list of phrases you wrote down in Activity 15. From your partner's list, choose the phrases you may need for writing your syllabus later in the unit and add them to your own.**

Lesson 2 A syllabus that works

Lead-in

1 Tick the statements about syllabus design that are true for you.

- I have written a syllabus in my mother tongue, but I have never written a syllabus in English.
- When I had to write a syllabus in English, I had to do it from scratch.
- I just filled in a template.
- I found a similar course on the internet and adapted its format and content to my needs.
- I translated the existing syllabus from my native language into English.

Listening

2 Work in pairs. Place the words in the pyramid. Explain the sequence.

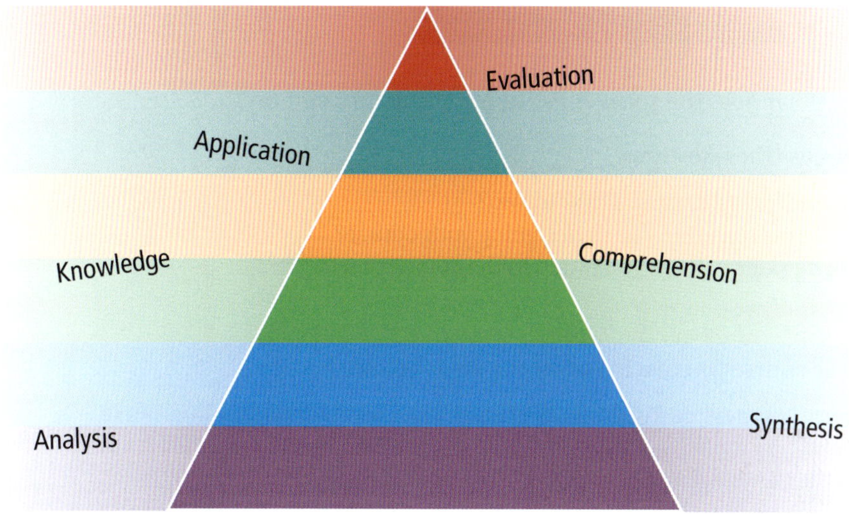

3 34 Listen to the first part of a presentation explaining an educational model and answer the questions below.

1 What is the full name of the model?
2 Who was the author of the model?
3 When was the model developed?
4 How many main domains are there in the model?
5 What is a taxonomy?

4 34 Listen again to check the sequence you created in Activity 2.

5 35 **Listen to the second part of the presentation. Look at the slide from the presentation and find two differences between the slide and what the speaker says.**

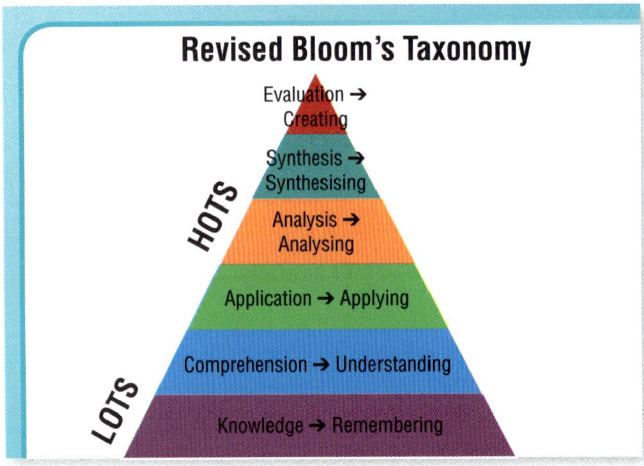

6 35 **Listen again. What does the speaker like about Bloom's taxonomy?**

7 Work in groups. Discuss the questions.

1 What information in the presentation is new to you?
2 How useful would Bloom's taxonomy be in designing your course?
3 What levels of thinking skills will/do you target in the course you teach?

Language focus

8 Write the aims of the course you teach. Follow the steps below.

1 Look again at Extract C on page 126 and identify the phrases used for describing course aims.
2 Add the phrases to the Language Support box.

Language Support: stating goals/aims

The course aims to (infinitive) ...
The course is aimed at verb+*ing*
____

The course has the following objectives: (1) ...
The overall goal of the course is ...
____

3 Use the phrases in the Language Support box to write your aims.

This programme aims to enhance participants' understanding of academic practice in higher education.

9 Read these sentences taken from course descriptions. Complete the table with phrases from them. The first one has been done for you.

1 The course equips students with knowledge about language description.
2 The course explores how Americans have confronted energy challenges since the end of World War II.
3 The course acquaints students with guidelines that help them create well-crafted academic communication.
4 The course focuses on a wide range of subjects within the field of education and related areas.

5 This course examines how and why communication evolved as a science.
6 This class develops students' skills in qualitative analysis and presentation.

Verb + something	Verb + *how* + clause	Verb + preposition + something	Verb + somebody + preposition
			equip students with

10 **Look again at Extract E on page 126 and add more phrases to the table.**

11 **Read the tips below on how to write the section in the syllabus on learning outcomes. Complete the gaps with the words in the box. The first one has been done for you.**

behaviour	knowledge	action verb	~~learning outcomes~~
attitudes	skills	achievement	purpose

Describing learning outcomes

- [1] *Learning outcomes* should describe what students should know or be able to do at the end of the course that they couldn't do before.
- When describing learning outcomes, focus on student performance, [2] ________ , and [3] ________ , not teacher activity.
- Good learning outcomes shouldn't be too abstract (e.g. 'the students will understand what good literature is'); too narrow (e.g. 'the students will know what a ground is'); or be restricted to lower-level cognitive skills (e.g. 'the students will be able to name the countries in Africa').
- Learning outcomes should support the overall [4] ________ of the course.
- Learning outcomes should be assessable.
- Experts often talk about using the abbreviation 'SKA' to frame learning outcomes for the course
  [5] ________ : what students should be able to do
  [6] ________ : what students should know and understand
  [7] ________ : what the students' opinions will be about the subject matter of the course by the time it is completed.
- Identify what the students should gain throughout the course by writing sentences that begin as follows
  By the end of the course, students will be able to …
  and then supplying a strong, [8] ________ .
- Words or phrases such as *know, think, learn, remember, understand, be aware of, be familiar with* and *have knowledge of* are NOT measurable and should be avoided.

12 **Read the examples of learning outcomes. In each example, underline the action verbs and the nouns that go with them. The first one has been done for you.**

1 Students will have acquired the skills of evaluating educational research critically.
2 Students will be able to use technology effectively in the delivery of instruction, assessment and professional development.
3 By the end of the course, students will have demonstrated the ability to describe the impact of research and other accomplishments in space technology based on scientific theories and principles.
4 Students will be able to explain a variety of electromagnetic phenomena in terms of a few relatively simple laws.
5 By the end of the course, students will be able to compare qualitative data systematically by selecting appropriate strategies.
6 Students will have demonstrated their familiarity with different ways of interpreting research findings.
7 Students will be able to design spam filtering software.

13 **This table summarises the categories in the revised version of Bloom's taxonomy. Put the verbs you underlined in Activity 12 into the appropriate column.**

Remembering	Understanding	Applying	Analysing	Evaluating	Creating
list find recognise ________	summarise exemplify classify ________ ________	carry out implement execute ________	structure arrange question ________	experiment test monitor ________	produce construct plan ________

14 **Work in pairs. Follow the steps below.**

1 Prepare six cards for your partner. On each card, write two questions about the subject you teach for each level of the revised version of Bloom's taxonomy. Use the verbs in Activity 13 where possible.

What research methods are used widely in the field of sociology?
Which research methods are most appropriate in sociology and why?

2 Read the questions on each of your partner's cards. Decide what level in the revised taxonomy they belong to. Check with your partner.

What research methods are used widely in the field of sociology? (remembering)
Which research methods are most appropriate in sociology and why? (evaluating)

Follow-up

15 **Prepare to write a draft of a course syllabus (maximum length: one page). It could be the one you named in Lesson 1 (see Activity 14 on page 128). Follow the steps below.**

1 Revise the language of Lessons 1 and 2 and the phrases you chose in Activity 15, Lesson 1 on page 128.
2 Write a draft of the syllabus. Focus only on Sections 1–6 that are in the list in Activity 10, Lesson 1 on page 125.
3 Edit and proofread your draft. Bring it to class.

16 **Work in pairs. Exchange the syllabuses you have written. Read your partner's syllabus and give feedback. Use the questions below as guidelines.**

- Are the goals clear?
- Can the learning outcomes be assessed?

Lesson 3 Assessment

Lead-in

1 Work in groups. Discuss the questions.

1 How many times have you been assessed professionally since your graduation from university?
2 Do you think you will be assessed in the future? If yes, how?

Reading

2 Read Text 1 and give it a title. Compare your title with your classmates' suggestions.

Text 1

Although there are very many assessment methods, the most commonly used in higher education still tend to be the essay and/or the traditional timed examination, either in the format of MCQs, (multiple choice questions) or short answers, or mathematical problems. Obviously, choosing an appropriate task to assess students' achievements is not easy. The primary goal is to set assessment tasks that support learning and help students to achieve the learning outcomes of the educational programme. In other words, the method of assessment should be relevant to the learning outcome it is supposed to test. For example, if we want to test students' ability to assess and manage information, then an annotated bibliography, a project or a dissertation would be appropriate, but if we are more concerned with students' communication skills, an oral presentation, a discussion, or a role play might be the best assessment options. Observation of real or simulated professional practice or a lab report can be relevant to evaluate science students' laboratory skills. Now computer-based assessment is increasingly being used in many institutions. It is thought to be motivating to students, enabling them to practise discipline-specific skills and abilities.

3 Which problem with assessment is mentioned in Text 1? Is it a problem for you?

4 Read Text 1 again and make a list of possible assessment tasks. You will need them later in the lesson.

Listening

5 ⊙36 Listen to a lecture on assessment and answer the questions.

1 What is the difference between formative and summative assessment?
2 What does the choice of an assessment task depend on?
3 What should students be clear about when they are assessed?

6 ⊙36 Listen again and add more assessment tasks to the list you started in Activity 4.

Language focus

7 **Read the phrases in the box. Classify them into two groups and give each group a heading.**

Could you stop there for a moment?
Could I just add that ...?
May I interrupt you for a moment?
Can I break in for a second?
I'd just like to point out that ...
Sorry for interrupting, but may I put in a word?
Before you go on, let me make a point ...
There's something else I'd like to say ...
I'd like to add that ...
What I'd also like to say is ...

8 **Work in groups. Go back to Activities 4 and 6 and put the assessment tasks on a continuum from more 'closed' (objective) types to more 'open' (subjective) types. While discussing where to put them, use the phrases in Activity 7.**

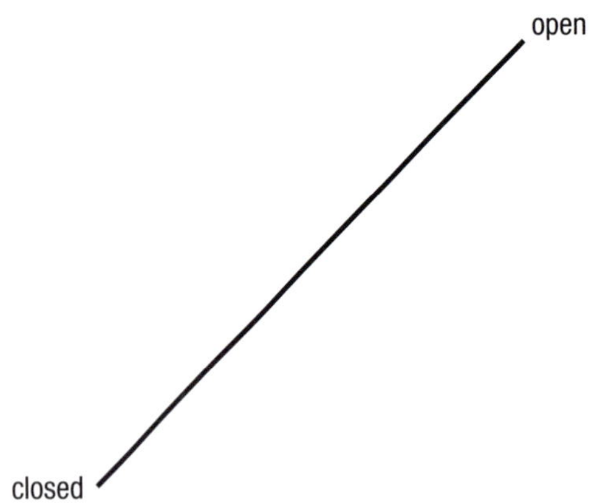

9 **Read these final learning outcomes and choose the most suitable assessment tasks from your list.**

By the end of the course students will demonstrate an ability

1 to develop software
2 to compare economic events
3 to determine the most effective strategy for a company entering an international market
4 to define the different medications according to their composition and applications
5 to apply formulae to mathematical problems

Reading

10 Read the extracts from different syllabi (A–C) and match them with courses 1–3.

1 Introduction to Programming
2 Financial Markets
3 Introduction to Public Speaking

A ____________________

Assessment methods will seek to relate current academic and practitioner thinking to the changing demands of financial markets.

The assessment tasks will include:

- a report on a case study (Module 1)
- a group presentation (Module 2)
- a research project (Module 3-5)

Students should demonstrate:

- evidence of the breadth of research supported with references to theory
- currency of thought
- evidence of critical reflection
- clarity of argument

B ____________________

Students' grades were based on the following scheme:

15% Lab average

5% Homework

30% Three programming projects

30% Three tests

20% Final examination

C ____________________

The course assignments and activities are:

Video lectures and follow-up quizzes: Most of the course content is delivered through video lectures focused on specific aspects of speaking in public. Quizzes are embedded after each video to reinforce basic knowledge of certain concepts and argument structures.

Samples Analysis: In order to refine their skills, students are required to examine and discuss sample speeches and speakers' behaviour. Discussion forums aim to facilitate sharing ideas and learning from your peers.

Peer Assessment Tasks: There are three options for a final course assignment: an impromptu, informative or persuasive speech. All students are asked to record and post videos of their speeches and also provide feedback on at least two speeches of their peers.

11 **Work in groups. Discuss the questions. Use phrases from Activity 7 in your discussion.**

1 What is assessed in each course: skills or knowledge?
2 What forms of assessment are used?
3 How do these three texts differ in their format? Why do you think they use different formats?
4 Compare these English-medium assessment specifications with those in your subject in your own language. What are the similarities and differences?
5 What tasks do you use to assess your students' achievement of learning outcomes?
6 In your subject, do you assess mainly knowledge or skills?

Language focus

12 **Read the samples generated by a concordancer. Answer the questions.**

concordancer: a software program that generates sentences with a particular word in them

1 What verb form follows *a means of, a way of* and *involve*?
2 What adverbs collocate with *evaluate*?
3 Can the verbs *assess* and *evaluate* be used without an object?
4 What verbs collocate with the noun *task*?

........a means of **assessing** the work of ....
........being able to **assess** data you 're ....
........communication skills are **assessed** and there 's ....
........reasonable way of **assessing** this exercise is ....
........that does involve **evaluating** board position ....
........should be formally **evaluated** before making a decision ....
........colleagues who will **evaluate** it critically ....
........after practising a **task** over and over ....
........perform both these **tasks** in order to ....
........depending on the **task** you have different ....
........group discussion **task** during class ....
........to do the **task** just talking through ....

13 **Imagine that you're teaching a class in English. What would you say in class if you wanted to explain**

- how students are going to be assessed at the end of the course?
- what knowledge/skill will be tested?

Use phrases from Activity 12, if appropriate. Start your explanations with

You're supposed to ...
You'll be required to ...
You'll have to ...
You'll be expected to ...
You should be able to ...

You'll have to find a means of assessing the effectiveness of the company decision.
You're supposed to do all the tasks assigned in the lab.

14 Work in groups. Try your instructions on the other members of your group. Ask them whether your explanations were clear. Use the language in the Language Support box.

Language Support: checking understanding / showing understanding

Checking understanding
Can you follow me?
Are you with me?
Are you all clear about what you have to do?

Lack of understanding
Sorry, I didn't get it.
It's not clear, I'm afraid.
Could you explain it again?

Showing understanding
I see.
I've got that.
OK/All right.
That's clear now.

Follow-up

15 Write the Assessment section in a syllabus for a course you teach. Use the language presented in this lesson.

16 Work in pairs. Share your Assessment section with your partner and ask for feedback.

Unit 3 Using English as the medium of instruction

By the end of this unit you will be able to
- write a post with an announcement of your course
- give definitions and instructions to students
- use the language of sequencing to describe the stages of preparation for a class you teach

Lesson 1 Presenting your syllabus

Lead-in

1 Work in groups. There is a trend nowadays in the global educational world to 'sell' institutional or an individual's courses online. Discuss the questions.

1 What is your attitude to this trend?
2 Is it necessary to have a blog or a personal/institutional site? What for?

Listening

2 37 Listen to a presentation of a course. Answer the questions.

1 When could this presentation have been made?
2 Who are the audience?
3 What is the purpose of the presentation?

3 37 Listen again. Complete the table about the course.

Course title	
Requirements	
Course length	
Types of assessment	
Type of course	
How to enrol	
Deadline for enrolment	

4 Work in groups. Discuss the questions.

- Do you think students will be motivated to take the course after the presentation? Why? / Why not?
- Have you ever presented your courses? If yes, what points did you highlight?

Reading

5 Read Text 1 quickly and answer the questions.

1 Where does this text come from?
2 What kind of text is it?
3 How many sections are there in it?

Text 1

Introduction to ecosystems

Gain an understanding of the natural world, how the web of life works, with illustrations from around the world.

ABOUT THE COURSE

If we don't grasp why ecosystems function, it becomes harder to determine possible reasons for when they don't, and makes it difficult to identify possible environmental threats to humans. In this course you will discover how organisms are linked together by complex interrelationships, how such links are studied and how the physical properties of a particular habitat interact with the organisms that inhabit it. Using case studies, you will come to learn how knowledge of ecosystems leads to understanding of their individual importance, and how they can be preserved.

All Open University Science courses presented on FutureLearn are produced with the kind support of Dangoor Education.

EDUCATORS

David Robinson

REQUIREMENTS

This course is intended for those with an interest in natural history, conservation or the environment and does not require any previous experience of studying these subjects.

SHARE

6 **Read Text 1 again and complete the sentences below in your own words.**

1 This course is suitable for ____.

2 Participants in the course will learn ______________________________________.

3 Case studies will show ____.

7 **Read Text 2. Compare Texts 1 and 2. Look at the sequence of information, layout, paragraphing and length. Are they similar or different? In what ways?**

Text 2

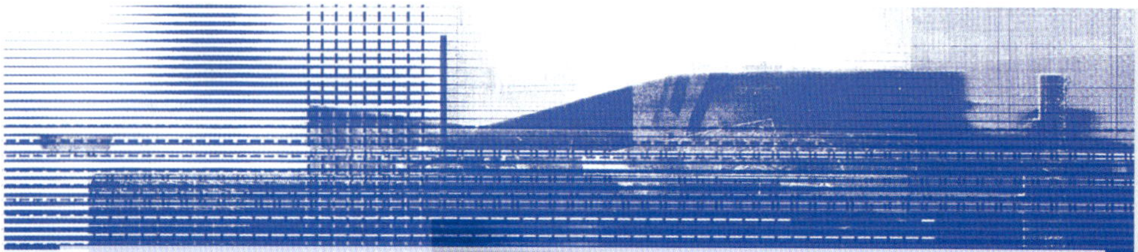

Web science: how the Web is changing the world

Explore how the Web has changed our world in the past 25 years and what might happen next.

ABOUT THE COURSE

You may be an avid user of the Web but this introductory course in Web Science will help you to understand the Web as both a social system and a technical system: a global information infrastructure built from the interactions of people and technologies.

We will examine the origins and evolution of the Web, and consider key questions of Security, Democracy, Networks and Economy from both computational and social science perspectives.

By following this course, you will have a greater understanding of the Web and begin to develop skills for the digital era – skills that are useful for everyday life and widely sought by the technology driven employers of today.

This is the start of a journey that could help you to shape the future of the World Wide Web.

8 **Work in pairs. Discuss the questions about Texts 1 and 2.**

1 What is the function of the section coming just after the title in both texts?
2 Which verb form occurs in this section? What is its function?

9 **Write one sentence to encourage students to enrol on your course. You can use verbs such as** ***join, find out, discover, learn, explore, uncover,*** **etc.**

10 **Read the extracts below from online advertisements for different courses. Write *AG* if the extract is from the attention-getter section, *I* if it is from the information about the course section or *ER* if it is from the enrolment requirements section.**

1 The course is pitched at first-year undergraduate level.
2 To prepare for the course, join us on Twitter or in blogging with the hashtag #FLsustain.
3 Everyone enrolled in Designing Cities will be expected to complete three assignments. These will be posted on the course site and they will be in the form of peer assessments.
4 Discover the basic fluid dynamics concepts behind aircraft analysis and design.
5 The course will combine video introductions, on-screen examples, articles and discussions to help you understand the principles behind computer programs.
6 Explore how to identify and develop great ideas into great companies.
7 Join us on an exploration to uncover new technology tools to connect your classroom and students to the Common Core.

Language focus

11 **Work in pairs. Fill in the gaps with the correct prepositions. Then go back to Texts 1 and 2 and check your answers.**

1 The course is intended ____________ intermediate-level students.
2 Have you read the introduction ____________ the third edition?
3 Tim did a three-year course ____________ linguistics at Newcastle.
4 The reason ____________ the disaster was engine failure, not human error.
5 The course will appeal to anyone with an interest ____________ world affairs.
6 He writes ____________ a Marxist perspective.
7 Reducing speed limits should lead ____________ fewer deaths on the roads.

12 **What verb form is underlined in Texts 1 and 2? Why is it used in the texts?**

13 **Read the Language Support box. Then complete sentences 1–6 with either *will* or *be going to* and the verbs in brackets.**

> **Language Support: *will* and *be going to* for predictions**
>
> ***Be going to*** is used to make firm predictions when there is a strong evidence for them, e.g. *It's going to rain.* (There are clouds in the sky.)
> ***Will*** is used to make predictions that aren't based on evidence, but may be true in the future, e.g. *I think he will get this grant.*
> In many cases, however, it is possible to use either *be going to* or *will*, e.g. *I don't think the present government will / is going to win the next election.*
> *Will* is more often used in writing. In speech, both *'ll* and *be going to* are used.

1 Look at all those students. The room ________________ (*be*) full for his lecture.
2 MOOC platforms ________________ (*allow*) students to connect directly with employers, I think.
3 It ________________ (*be*) a difficult meeting. There are lots of problems to discuss.
4 His presentation ________________ (*attract*) a lot of people. The title is so catchy.
5 She She isn't enjoying her work. I think she ________________ (*leave*) the university.
6 National authorities ________________ (*recognise*) international qualifications, I hope.

Follow-up

14 Imagine that you have been asked to promote your course on MOOC. Write a post with an announcement of your course (maximum 180 words). Follow the structure below. Use phrases from the texts and activities in this lesson. You can refer to the syllabus you have written in Unit 2. Remember, however, that the style here is less formal.

- the course title
- an attention-getter
- some brief information about the course
- the enrolment requirements

15 Work in pairs. Give the text of your announcement to your partner. Provide feedback to each other using the questions below as guidelines.

- Is the text clear?
- Is the information interesting?
- Is the language accurate?
- Are all the structural elements included?

Lesson 2 Giving definitions and instructions

Lead-in

1 Read the definitions and say what is wrong with them.

- Transformation is a kind of way of making one thing look like another.
- Company acquisition is when one company acquires another.
- A quince is a type of apple that people make jam with.

2 How often do you give definitions in your classes? What do you usually have to define?

Writing

3 Work in pairs. Read three definitions of the word *curriculum* and identify patterns for definitions.

- A curriculum is a document which lists and describes all the subjects learned in a school, college or university.
- A curriculum is a document listing and describing all the subjects learned in a school, college or university.
- A curriculum is a document designed to list and describe all the subjects learned in a school, college or university.

4 Complete definitions 1–6. Use the given words in the same order, adding appropriate phrases from the Language Support box below. The first one has been done for you.

1 physics /matter and energy /effect
Physics is the study of matter and energy and their effect on each other.
2 a project / a subject / a period of time
______
3 Cu / chemical / copper
______
4 a portfolio / documents / represent / somebody's work
______
5 a blog / online diary / someone / express views / record experiences
______
6 assessment / evaluate / somebody's work
______
7 a barometer / measure / atmospheric pressure
______

Language Support: defining

X is a kind/sort of ...	X is the symbol for ...
X is the study of ...	X is a means of verb+*ing*
X is a collection of ...	X is a device used for verb+*ing*
X is an element of/for ...	X is an instrument of/for verb+*ing*

5 Write definitions of three key terms from the subject you teach. Use the three different patterns in Activity 3.

6 Work in pairs. Read out your definitions from Activity 5 without saying the terms. (Just start with *It is* ...) Ask your partner to guess the terms. If necessary, try several times. Use the phrases from the Language Support box below.

Language Support: asking for clarification and clarifying

Asking for clarification	Clarifying
Can it be defined as ...?	In other words ...
Sorry, could you say that in a different way?	To put it another way ...
Are you saying that ...?	What I'm trying to say is ...

Reading

7 Work in pairs. Read these tips for giving instructions and rank them from the least important (1) to the most important (7).

Text 1

How to give instructions

You will need to have a repertoire of ways of giving instructions in practical classes such as workshops, lab work, etc. The development of this skill of giving instructions will also be relevant to you if you want to make your lectures more interactive. Effective instructions will help your students to better understand what you expect them to do.

1 Think of different techniques to attract students' attention, for example clapping your hands or knocking on a desk.
2 The best way to tell students how to do something is to actually do it yourself.
3 Always give instructions in the same language. Use commonly used words and short, simple sentences.
4 Avoid multi-layered instructions. Instructions should be divided into small chunks according to the different phases of the task that students have to perform.
5 Choose where to stand in the room when giving directions, for example stand close to the students who have difficulty in following you. In this way, you will be able to control them.
6 Check for understanding by asking questions related to the instructions.
7 Make the instructions sound polite. Use modal verbs and imperatives appropriately.

8 Work in groups. Discuss the order in which you have put the tips in Text 1.

Listening

9 **Read the list of phrases below and identify the function (a–c) of each. Put the letter of the function next to each phrase.**

1 Before you begin, you should ...
2 I would start by ...
3 After that, ...
4 Once you've done that, then ...
5 To begin with, ...
6 What I'd like you to do is ...
7 When you finish that, then ....
8 You'll have to ...

a explain the task in general terms
b explain how to get started
c explain how to continue

10 38 **Listen to the explanation of how ed.ted.com works. Put the steps below in the order the speaker mentions them.**

- Find a suitable video
- Create a discussion
- Set the context or learning objectives
- Register
- Check comprehension
- Add articles, references, links, etc.

11 38 **Listen to the explanation again. Add the phrases that the speaker uses to Activity 9.**

12 **Work in groups. Discuss the questions.**

1 Would you like to use ed.ted.com in teaching your subject in English? Why? / Why not?
2 How can students benefit from such classes?
3 What are the advantages and disadvantages for a teacher?
4 What similar online tools do you use in your classes?

Reading

13 **Read Text 2. Answer the questions.**

1 Where might this text appear?
2 Who are the instructions intended for?

Text 2

Registration

ALL new students must register online and full-time students must also confirm their attendance in person.

1. Online registration
Online registration opens three weeks before your start date. To register you should go to the university web portal.

Log on with the temporary username and password you used for the Applicant's Portal. If you were not given your temporary username and password you [1] ______________, contact the Student IT Helpline by email or phone. Contact details are on the back page of this booklet.

You will be shown a series of screens and asked to confirm or amend the details the University holds for you. At the end of the process (there may be a delay of up to 24 hours) you will be issued with your University username and password which will allow you access to all the University's Information Services, including email.

2. Full-time students
Full-time students [2] ______________ also confirm their attendance in person to complete the registration process. Full details of this process are available on the University's registration webpage.

14 **Read Text 2 again. Answer the question.**

How is the language of this written instruction different from the language in the explanation you listened to in Activity 10?

Language focus

15 **Read the Language Support box below. Fill in the gaps in Text 2 with the modal verbs *must* and *should*.**

Language Support: *must* and *should*

The modal verb *must* expresses obligation and is often used in regulations, e.g. *You must always follow the safety rules when working in the lab.*

The modal verb *should* is used to make recommendations, e.g. *You should use an up-to-date anti-virus program on your computer.*

16 **Read the sentences below and decide whether they are obligations or recommendations. Then fill in the gaps with *must* or *should*. Use the negative forms, if necessary.**

1 Laboratory equipment ______________ be renewed regularly, if finance permits.
2 All students ______________ read the document regarding emergency procedures prior to the first laboratory class.
3 You ______________ keep the work area clear of all materials except those needed for your work.
4 You ______________ wash your hands thoroughly after a lab session.
5 You ______________ eat, drink or smoke while working in the laboratory.
6 You ______________ be careful not to draw too many conclusions from a single experiment.
7 You ______________ look into any laser beam. It's dangerous.
8 You ______________ read the labels carefully.
9 You ______________ wait until the same experiment has been successfully replicated.

17 **From the list below, choose two situations suitable for your class. Think of an instruction for each situation. Use the tips in Activity 7.**

1 Draw students' attention to a visual and say what to do with it.
2 Refer students to the list of background reading and say what to do with it.
3 Ask students to work in pairs/groups and set a task.
4 Ask students to submit a paper/task by a certain deadline.
5 Ask students to start finish an activity.
6 Ask students to pay attention to a definition and ask them to write it down.
7 Any other situation that arises in your teaching context.

18 **Work in groups. Take turns and try your instructions out on each other.**

Follow-up

19 **Prepare some instructions (lasting 1–2 minutes) for your students. Choose an option below which is appropriate for the subject you teach. Use the language of the lesson.**

- Give some detailed instructions for a lab activity.
- Set a task for a seminar.
- Put students into groups for a project and explain what they have to do.
- Show students how to use a web tool.
- Instruct students in any other situation that arises in your teaching context.

20 **Work in groups. Take turns to give your instructions. Your classmates will play the role of students and ask you questions.**

Lesson 3 Planning makes perfect

Lead-in

1 Work in groups. Discuss the questions.

1 Have you ever taught a class that was totally unplanned?
2 If so, what was the result?

Language focus

2 Match the types of class (1–6) with their descriptions (a–f).

1 lecture	**a** a way of teaching through informal interaction in a group of about 20 students; a group discussion allows deeper investigation of the topic; students are asked to present their views on certain topics
2 seminar	**b** a way of teaching that allows more individual student attention; arranged as a small 'class' or an individual consultation with a teacher; it often has a specific focus, e.g. a close study of a text
3 workshop	**c** practical work conducted by a student or a group of students outside, rather than in a laboratory or in class
4 tutorial	**d** a formal presentation to a large group of students; a way of conveying information about a subject, usually with the use of visual aids and handouts; students take notes and ask questions
5 lab work	**e** working on practice-oriented assignments which are usually scheduled after lectures and discussions; students work under the supervision of a teacher or on their own; usually devoid of any kind of discussion
6 fieldwork	**f** a teaching session often with a practical focus; it is likely to involve hands-on activity around a task as well as structured group work; students engage in intensive discussion of a particular subject or project

3 Work in groups. Discuss the questions.

1 Which of these types of class do you use in your course?
2 Which of them do your students find most effective?

Listening

4 39 Listen to a lecturer in intercultural communication talking about how she prepares for a lecture. Number the steps below in the order she mentions them.

- identifying students' needs and interests
- choosing types of activities
- observing and collecting real-life ideas
- thinking of ways of involving students
- background reading

5 Work in pairs. Discuss the questions.

1 How often do you have to improvise during a lecture? When do you improvise?
2 How is the balance between preparation and improvisation different when you lecture in your own language and when you teach through the medium of English?

6 Work in groups. Share ideas on how you prepare for a lecture. Start your sentences with the phrases below.

- What I usually do is ...
- What works very well for me is ...
- I think that the most effective way is ...

Reading

7 Read the statements and tick the column which is true for you.

Statement	always	often	sometimes	never
1 I use different visuals in my classes.				
2 I give handouts of my lectures before the class.				
3 Before the class I post tasks and my presentation online.				
4 I ask students to take notes in class.				
5 I give students background reading before the class.				

8 Read the first and the last paragraphs of a blog post below (Text 1) quickly. Identify the research topic and its major results. Why are these parts of the text important?

Text 1

Wednesday, 7 July, 2010

therefore rather than by contrast

The common-sense arguments for and against providing students with slide handouts before a lecture are well rehearsed. Having the handouts means students need take fewer notes, [1] ________ allowing them to sit back and actually listen to what's said. Withholding the handouts, [2] ________, encourages students to make more notes, perhaps ensuring that they're more engaged with the lecture material [3] ________ mind-wandering.

even when still however

'The data reported here represent only a first step and do not resolve this issue,' the researchers concluded. 'In no case, [4] ________, did having the handouts during a lecture impair performance on the final tests. [5] ________ there were no differences in final test performance, students [6] ________ benefited in the sense that they reached the same level of learning with less work.'

rehearse: repeat

impair: make worse

9 Read Text 1 again. Fill in the gaps with the words in the boxes. Why are they necessary?

10 Read the main body of the blog post (Text 2) quickly. What do these numbers refer to?

1 74% **2** 50% **3** 21% **4** 29% **5** 12 minutes

Text 2

A To find out what really works better, Marsh and Sink had several dozen students watch a few 12-minute videos of real-life PowerPoint science lectures. Sometimes they were given the handouts for use during the lecture; other times the handouts were only provided later. Half the students were subsequently tested on the lecture material after a 12-minute delay; the other students were tested a week later. In both cases, a few minutes before testing, the students were allowed to review their own notes and the handouts (for some of the lectures, this was the first time the handouts were provided). The key finding is that having handouts in the lecture versus only receiving them at the review stage made no difference to test performance. Although the students who had the handouts in-lecture made fewer notes, this didn't harm their test performance at either the 12-minute or 1-week delay.

B The findings provide preliminary evidence that lecturers should provide their students with handouts during the lecture. Regarding the more extensive note-taking that took place when handouts were held back until after a lecture, the researchers speculated that this was 'unlikely to be a deep encoding task', which would normally be expected to aid memory retention, and may instead have acted merely as a distraction.

C A follow-up study with 34 students was identical to the first but the testing only took place 12 minutes after the lectures and this time the review session was self-paced for half the students but just two-minutes long for the others. Students provided with handouts during the lectures again took fewer notes but this time they actually out-performed those who only received the handouts after the lectures.

D Elizabeth Marsh and Holli Sink began their investigation of this issue by surveying university students and lecturers. The student verdict was clear: 74 per cent said they preferred to be given slide handouts prior to the lecture, the most commonly cited reason being that having the handouts helps with note-taking. The lecturers were more equivocal. Fifty per cent said they preferred to provide handouts prior to the lecture, but 21 per cent said they never gave out handouts and 29 per cent preferred to distribute afterwards. The most common lecturer reason for retaining handouts was students wouldn't pay attention if they had the handouts.

equivocal: having opposing opinions

retain: keep

11 Read Text 2 again and put the paragraphs in the logical order. Underline the phrases that helped you do this.

12 Work in groups. Go back to Activity 6 on page 149. How are your answers different from the research results in Text 1? Are you for or against giving handouts in advance? Give your reasons.

Language focus

13 Go back to Texts 1 and 2. Find all the verbs that can be used with the word *handout.* Which of the phrases can you use in the classroom?

14 Imagine that you're teaching a class in English. What would you say in class if you wanted to

- ask students to pass the handouts around
- refer students to Task 3 on the handouts
- refer students to page 1 on the handouts
- have the handouts back
- ask learners not to write on the handouts.
-

Start your instructions with *Could you ...* , *I'd like you to ...* , *Will you, please, ...* .

15 Find phrases from Text 2 that have similar meanings to the phrases below. You will need this sequencing language in the next activity.

- to start something with
- before
- after
- all through a particular period

Follow-up

16 Prepare to present a flowchart demonstrating the stages of preparation for your class (lecture, lab, seminar, etc). Follow the steps below.

1 Go back to Activities 4–6 for ideas.
2 Create a flowchart. Write short notes and indicate the sequence of stages with symbols, e.g. arrows.
3 Add useful language from other modules to sequence the steps and to refer to visuals. Use language from Activity 15 in this lesson.

17 Work in groups. Present the flowchart and answer your classmates' questions.

Unit 4 Giving a lecture in English

By the end of this unit you will be able to
- use language appropriately to structure and deliver part of a lecture in English
- develop the language you need to interact with students during a lecture
- use English for classroom management

Lesson 1 Why do we lecture?

Lead-in

1 Complete the quotation below with the adjectives in the box.

great	mediocre	good	superior

The [1] ______________ teacher tells. The [2] ______________ teacher explains. The [3] ______________ teacher demonstrates. The [4] ______________ teacher inspires. (William Arthur Ward)

2 Work in pairs. Compare your answers and discuss the questions.

1 Do you agree with the quotation?
2 How would you define a good university teacher?

Listening

3 Work in groups. Draw up a list of skills a teacher needs to cope with changes and new challenges in education.

4 ⊙40 Listen to two teachers and make notes in the table on the skills they mention.

	Skills
Teacher 1	
Teacher 2	

5 Work in the same groups as in Activity 3. Compare your notes. Are the speakers' answers similar to yours in Activity 3? Which of the skills are most important, in your opinion, and why?

Language focus 1

6 ⊙40 Fill in the prepositions in the sentences. Listen again to check your answers.

1 Actually, technology has allowed everyone, ______________ social networks, to engage ______________ what's called 'cooperative intelligence'.
2 We shouldn't be afraid ______________ taking risks and failing sometimes.
3 Just standing ______________ them and talking ______________ them about the subject does not mean that they're learning anything.
4 Every teacher should be ready to learn ______________ every lesson and to be as good ______________ learning as ______________ teaching.
5 A teacher asks questions and involves learners ______________ thinking.

Reading

7 **Read Text 1. Answer the three questions at the end of the text. Then work in pairs and discuss your answers. Give your reasons.**

Text 1

For centuries, the lecture has been the most economical way to 'educate' a large number of students. Since it was first employed in Plato's Academy, the lecture, which emphasises knowledge delivery from the teacher to students as the purpose of education, has been favoured as the dominant teaching model across the globe. Recently, this time-honoured method has come under attack for preventing interaction between students and the professor. Also its ability to foster higher order thinking skills is being challenged. Is this age-old model of learning sufficient to prepare students for tomorrow? Are lectures less effective than active learning techniques in promoting students' learning? Should the lecture be replaced with the newer, more 'active' methods?

Language focus 2

8 **Find words and phrases in Text 1 that are similar in meaning to the words and phrase below.**

1 use (v)
2 stress (v)
3 prefer
4 proved by tradition
5 develop
6 substitute (by)

9 **The words in italics in the sentences below are misplaced. Correct them using words from Activity 8.**

1 Electrons in atoms can be *emphasised by* muons.
2 Another alternative for solving the problem is to *foster* the principle of minimal change.
3 These figures *employ* the importance of protecting these habitats.
4 The course is designed to *favour* language skills.
5 Students usually *replace* particular types of interactive learning, for example, debates.

Reading

10 Read the conversation between two university teachers quickly and answer the questions.

1 What is the 'flipped classroom'?
2 What higher order thinking skills does the 'flipped classroom' target?
3 Does the 'flipped classroom' really improve student performance?

Text 2

A: [1] *Everyone seems to be talking about 'flipping' their classroom these days. What's it all about?*

B: Actually, it's something I've also been experimenting with. Most of the literature and research on it seems to come from America, but it's attracting interest over here too. I picked up the idea at a conference last year, at a presentation by a Californian physicist. He claimed to have noticed significant improvements in his students' engagement with learning by turning his existing practice on its head.

A: [2] ______________________

B: Well, instead of transmitting knowledge through a standard lecture and then leaving students to work out applications for themselves, he provides the basic input *before* his classes through a combination of reading and video lectures.

A: [3] ______________________

B: Yes, the material is all made available on the university's learning platform – Moodle or whatever – and the students are expected to access it and come to the class prepared.

A: [4] ______________________

B: Good question! The class itself is centred on discussion, problem-solving and lots of questioning aimed at getting students to think critically about what they have learned. The students can really only engage in all this if they already have some basic subject knowledge.

A: [5] ______________________

B: Absolutely. The emphasis is on developing students' higher order thinking skills – you know, as defined in the revision of Bloom's taxonomy – getting them to apply knowledge to the solving of problems, for example, to analyse issues, synthesise ideas and to create new meanings for themselves, rather than just relying on others. In a way it's about developing a research mentality in them through engaging them actively in addressing challenging questions and formulating questions of their own. One guy who the presenter quoted – Mazur, I think he was called – gives mini-lectures, then uses conceptual questions in class, and the students have to answer by clicking on a hand-held device. He sees the results in percentage terms immediately and if fewer than 65% give a right answer he immediately engages the class in small group discussion of the question to enable them to reconsider it and go deeper. Again promoting higher order thinking.

A: [6] ______________________

B: There's no research yet to prove that this is the case, only anecdotal evidence from proponents, but I have to say that the students in my third-year microbiology class are definitely more engaged and motivated, and that's got to be good ...

proponent: someone who speaks publicly in support of an idea

11 Read Text 2 again and write teacher A's questions in the box below in the correct place. The first one has been done for you.

> I see … but prepared for what?
> That sounds intriguing, but what does it mean in practice?
> But how do we know that this really improves student performance?
> ~~Everyone seems to be talking about 'flipping' their classroom these days. What's it all about?~~
> So there's a bit of learning technology involved?
> That seems like quite a radical shift in teaching method.

12 Work in pairs. Look at flowcharts A and B. Which of them refers to traditional lecturing and which one to flipped classes? Complete the boxes with your notes from Texts 1 and 2.

Flowchart A

Input: ____________________

↓

Main class activities: listening, taking notes

↓

Knowledge assimilation: doing homework after class

Flowchart B

Input: ____________________

↓

Main class activities: ____________________

↓

Knowledge assimilation: answering conceptual questions in class

13 Work in groups. Discuss the advantages and disadvantages of both the traditional and the flipped classroom. Use your notes from Activity 12. Do you use a flipped classroom in teaching your subject? If not, would you like to try it? Why? / Why not?

Language focus

14 **Tick the features that make Text 2 conversational. Find examples in the text to illustrate these features.**

- full verb forms
- phrasal verbs
- incomplete sentences
- phrases of opinion
- formal vocabulary
- responses showing understanding
- phrases of agreement
- contracted verb forms
- informal vocabulary
- questions and answers
- complete sentences

15 **Replace the underlined words and phrases in the sentences below with phrasal verbs from the box.**

pick something up	work out	take in	turn on their head

1 How is your new series of lectures developing?
2 It was an interesting lecture but there was just too much to absorb.
3 He hadn't done any Skyping before, but he learned really quickly.
4 These new findings made people think about the accepted theories in a completely different way.

16 **Work in pairs. Match the lecturer's questions (1–6) to with the reasons for asking them (a–f).**

1 Can you give us an example of what you mean?
2 Does this always happen?
3 Why do you support this idea?
4 Is there another way of looking at this?
5 How will it affect the environment?
6 Why do you think I asked this question?

a to probe reasons and evidence
b to question a point of view
c to clarify a concept
d to encourage reflection
e to challenge assumptions
f to examine consequences

17 **Work in groups. Discuss what kind of questions you usually ask your students and what kind of questions students like most. Explain why.**

Follow-up

18 **Start preparing for a lecture (traditional or 'flipped') that you are going to deliver at the end of this unit. Follow the steps below.**

1 Think of the topic of your lecture.
2 Decide which part of a lecture (lasting 7–10 minutes) in your specialism you are going to simulate, e.g.
   - presenting a classification
   - explaining and illustrating a concept/theory
   - presenting a controversial issue
   - describing a visual
   - giving a task or advice on readings
   - any other situation that arises in your teaching context
3 Draft a plan. Share your plan with a partner and give each other feedback.
4 Collect materials. Think of appropriate examples, statistics and illustrations of the ideas.
5 Refer to the list of purposes in Activity 16. Prepare two questions for each of these purposes to ask your students at the right moment in your session.

Lesson 2 An effective lecture

Lead-in

1 Have you ever fallen asleep in a lecture or seen other people do so? If so, why did it happen? Work in groups and share your experiences.

Reading

2 Read these students' posts on a forum (below and on page 158), answering the question 'What's your attitude to lectures?' Make notes on their positive and negative attitudes.

positive: great delivery
negative: lecturers read, not speak

1 Most of the time, lectures **suck**. Best sleeping pill. Professors reciting their own textbooks that I can read myself (but don't really want to). In the seminar format, you – sometimes – have an opportunity to talk to the professor and to your classmates, which is conducive to learning something; it doesn't even matter what you talk about. I remember reading one sentence of Plato and discussing it for the rest of the class. However, I've heard a few great lectures, delivered by individuals who simply had something to share. In those cases the format didn't matter; I sat there completely taken by a personality, or a story, and could feel things going through my mind and just changing my world view.

2 Interesting, we're rarely asked which type of lectures we'd like to have, but should such a chance arise, I'd definitely choose interactive lectures. Just receiving information, not being emotionally involved, is useless. U don't have the feeling that u need the info. I like it when a lecturer invites a specialist in this field, a practitioner, to speak. It becomes clear why we learn all this stuff. I guess a lecture shouldn't be boring even if the subject is not very exciting. Jokes, real-life examples, slides and video can help students stay focused. And of course, the manner of presentation: the voice, expressing emotions. I like teachers who are good narrators.

suck: be unpleasant

3 You know, I can't confidently say if I'm for or against lectures as a type of teaching. It's a waste of time if a teacher stays in their place, looks at their papers and reads all the materials in a quiet, monotonous voice. No eye contact, no interaction with students. But when a lecturer is interested in their subject their eyes sparkle, they present their information in a lively way, talk to students, ask leading questions and tell interesting stories. Students always come to such lectures, even if the teacher doesn't make a note of attendance. If only all lecturers were like this ...

4 Many students I know skip the lectures of some teachers 'cause there's nothing new or different from what they can learn from the coursebook. And UR always asking yourself why can't we just get those materials & read them at home. Seems the most efficient way 2 study is 2 make students think. Otherwise lectures become natter when students've nothing 2 do, only listening, or texting or googling sth. Monotonous lectures are weary for those who come 2 listen, 2 discover, not just 2 attend.

natter: talk for a long time without any purpose

5 In many universities, lecturing is the most common teaching method. In my opinion, it is the best way to get facts across. A teacher can give a lot of information during the lecture without wasting time on discussion and practice. Besides, in lectures students are able to get information that we can't get from other sources.

3 Work in pairs. Put the words in the correct order to make a list of tips on how to make a lecture effective.

1 students / Find / about / out / topic. / what / know / the

______

2 during / the / Check / lecture. / understanding

______

3 them / give / Ask / a / and / question / to / time / discuss / it. / students

______

4 more / six / Present / than / points. / no / main

______

5 your / Use / support / ideas. / visuals / to

______

6 concepts / examples / Use / vivid / related / the / explain. / to / you

______

7 to / Refer / online / learners / to / knowledge. / resources / expand / and / printed / their

______

8 explaining / Involve / some / students / in / illustrating / or / points.

______

9 and / answer / Leave / for / sessions. / question / time

______

10 platforms, / technology: / etc. / online / presentation/ videos, / Use / tools,

______

4 Work in groups. Rank the tips in Activity 3 from the least important (1) to the most important (10). Discuss your choices.

5 Work in groups. Go back to Activities 2 and 3 and make a list of criteria for an effective lecture. You will need these later in Activity 10.

Listening

6 41 Listen to the beginning of a lecture on nonverbal communication. Put the steps below in the order you hear them.

- giving a definition
- greeting the audience
- giving an interesting fact to emphasise the importance of the topic
- introducing the topic
- probing what students know about the topic

7 42 Listen to another part of the lecture and answer the questions.

1 What does the lecturer want students to learn?
2 How is the lecture organised?

8 42 Listen to the extract again and fill in the gaps with words signalling classification.

There is quite a range of [1] ______________ of nonverbal communication. All nonverbal messages can be [2] ______________ into four major [3] ______________ . They are: kinesics, paralanguage, proxemics and image. These four groups in their turn [4] ______________ several [5] ______________ ...

Gestures also [7] ______________ the category of kinesics as well as the subcategory of oculesics …

The second [8] ______________ of nonverbal messages is paralanguage, which includes voice quality, its … hm … colour and style, as well as prosodic features such as rhythm, intonation and stress. …

Let's turn to the third [9] ______________ , proxemics, or territoriality …

And the last [10] ______________ of nonverbal messages for today is image or object communication ...

9 Work in groups. Discuss the questions.

- What information in the lecture was new to you?
- How important is this information to you as a lecturer?
- What aspects of nonverbal communication do you think you need to develop?

10 Work in groups. Go back to the list of criteria for an effective lecture that you made in Activity 5. Evaluate the lecture you have listened to, using your criteria. Share your ideas with other groups.

Language focus

11 Match the phrases that can be used in the classroom (1–6) with their functions (a–f).

1	This is the most crucial step of the process. It is especially important to know that ... There are three absolutely essential points that need to be made.	**a**	to finish a class
2	The idea of this task is to ... Let's start with a look at the difficulties in the ... What does it mean in this context?	**b**	to offer help
3	Who needs help? I'll help you if you get stuck. Let me know if you run into a problem.	**c**	to highlight key points
4	Good. I think we can leave it there for a while. OK. Finally, a brief word about next Monday. Thank you for the class. Goodbye.	**d**	to manage a class
5	Right. Now we'll do some group work. Could you discuss it in pairs, please? Could you work on your own first?	**e**	to explain
6	Interesting! Could you say more? Not bad! Any other suggestions? Great! That's the way to go. Carry on as you have been doing. Well done.	**f**	to encourage students

12 43 Listen to the conclusion of the lecture on nonverbal communication. Tick the elements that are part of the conclusion.

- a summary of the main points
- new information
- highlighting the importance of the topic
- a question-and-answer session
- warning against generalisations
- giving a task
- checking understanding

13 Work in groups. Discuss the questions.

1 How do you usually finish your lectures?
2 Why is a summary an important part of a conclusion?
3 What phrases do you use to signal the conclusion?

Follow-up

14 In Lesson 1 you started planning a lecture. Now give some more thought to it by following the steps below.

1 Write a draft of your lecture. Ask your English teacher for help if necessary.
2 Decide on the classroom language you may need to use. Review the phrases from Activity 11 above and in Unit 3 (see Activity 9 on page 145 and Activity 14 on page 151).
3 Prepare visuals if necessary.

Lesson 3 Students' involvement

Lead-in

1 **Work in pairs. Complete the Chinese proverb below with the verbs in the box. Compare your answers with other pairs.**

remember	tell	involve	forget	show	learn

1 ____________ me and I'll 2 ____________ . 3 ____________ me and I'll 4 ____________ .
5 ____________ me and I'll 6 ____________ .

2 **Work in groups. Discuss the question below.**

Do you agree that all students learn your subject better if they interact with each other and the teacher? Why? / Why not?

Reading

3 **Read Text 1 and fill in the gaps with phrases a–f below.**

a use a show of hands to check the responses
b build rapport with the students by chatting to them
c pose a challenging question
d allow you to shift students' attention
e show students a video clip
f use demonstrations

Text 1

There are quite a number of ways to involve students in the learning process. One of them, which can be exploited even before your lecture starts, is to 1 ____________________ . Make sure that the students know how to contact you after the class if they want to discuss something with you.

Secondly, the lecture may be engaging by the very fact that is it well organised and interesting. No matter how well intentioned and motivated, students can stay focused only for about 15–20 minutes. When you plan your classes, add activities that 2 ____________________ .

The third and probably the most important aspect of student engagement is their active participation in the lecture. There is a variety of ways, but here are a few common ones, particularly suitable for large classes.

- 3 ____________________ . Ask students to discuss it in small groups and then take feedback from a few groups to hear what they think.
- 4 ____________________ and ask students to look for specific facts/ quotations that support particular arguments. You might ask all students to address the same argument or different students to look at different arguments.
- Ask the students to vote on the right answer to a multiple-choice question (MCQ). 5 ____________________ , or use an electronic voting system.
- 6 ____________________ that can involve students directly.

Of course, this list can be continued. All teachers have their tricks of the trade.

4 **Work in groups. Discuss the questions.**

- Which of the techniques in Text 1 might be useful to teach your subject matter?
- Which activities do you often use?
- Which of the activities practised by your classmates would you like to try?

Language focus

5 **Match the phrases that can be used in the classroom (1–4) with their functions (a–d).**

1 Raise your hand if you think it's right. Did you all find the same answer? Is everything clear?	**a** to share a fact or a story
2 It may surprise you to know that ... There's an interesting story about this. Do you know that ...	**b** to check understanding
3 You have five minutes to complete this. I expect you to finish the task in five minutes. Your time is up now, I am afraid.	**c** to respond to answers
4 That's right. Absolutely. Good try ... Any other views?	**d** to set a time limit

Reading

6 **The acronym 'INTRO' is used to describe the five-step process for starting a lecture. Guess which word each letter stands for. (Tip: all of them are nouns.)**

7 **Read Text 2 and check if your guesses were correct.**

Text 2

The beginning of the lecture is often the most important part of the session as it sets the tone for the students' response and receptivity. A poor introduction can turn the students off while a good introduction can make even the dullest subject engaging. The 'INTRO' mnemonic is particularly helpful to introduce the session.

I ____________ State something interesting to gain learners' attention: break the ice with an anecdote highlighting the importance of the topic; refer to a topical issue that is relevant to the lecture material or pose a question that the lecture will ultimately resolve.

N ____________ Establish the need for learning. Demonstrate why and how the lecture is important to the students. This includes making reference to the relevance of the material to the examination, but also, and of course more importantly, the actual practical application of the ideas and concepts to be covered.

T ____________ Specify the time frame. Make clear how the session time will be organised between various elements: lecture, activities, review of the previous week's exercises, and so on.

R ____________ Explain the range of the session. Make clear what will be covered during the lecture and what topics are left for self-study.

O ____________ It is also significant that students are aware of your aims and of the learning outcomes they are expected to achieve as a result of the engagement with the topic of the lecture.

8 Match words 1–7 with words a–g that are close in meaning.

1 anecdote	**a** accomplish
2 actual	**b** outcome
3 demonstrate	**c** story
4 result	**d** be aware of
5 achieve	**e** significant
6 important	**f** real
7 know	**g** show

9 Choose suitable words from Activity 8 to complete the sentences.

1 We expected 50 people, but the ______________ number was a lot higher.
2 It's too early to predict the ______________ of the meeting.
3 Mark wasn't ______________ of the risks at the time.
4 This research is based on ______________ , not fact.
5 The results of the experiment are not statistically ______________ .

Listening

10 44 Listen to the extracts from lectures (1–3) and match them with the attention getters (a–e) the lecturers use.

Lecture	
1	
2	
3	

a asking questions
b physical involvement
c giving a task to be completed by the end of the lecture
d using a visual
e referring to the previous lecture

11 44 Listen to the extracts again. Fill in the table with the phrases matching each heading. The first one has been done for you.

Giving an outline	*I'm going to explain ...*
Inviting students to review previous material	
Referring to visuals	

Language focus

12 Put the words in the correct order to make phrases that can be used to start a lecture.

1 about ... / I'm / talk / Today / going to

2 Can / have / please? / your / I / attention

3 important / because ... / This / is / lecture

4 we / start / today / with ... / don't / Why

5 end / you / be / of / will / By / the / able / lecture / the / to ...

13 Work in groups. Discuss the questions.

- How do you usually start your lectures?
- Which of the techniques described in this lesson would work in your context?
- What other techniques can be used to raise students' interest in your lectures?

Follow-up

14 Prepare to deliver a 7–10 minute part of the lecture you have been working on in this unit. Think about how you are going to involve the audience. Use the 'INTRO' principle at the beginning. Review the classroom English you may need to use. (See Activity 16 on page 156, Activity 11 on page 160 and Activity 5 on page 162.)

15 Before finishing your preparation, check if you are going to

- signal the start and the end of the lecture, and use transitions
- use interactive techniques to involve students
- use visuals to support your ideas
- use appropriate classroom English
- give clear instructions
- check understanding.

16 Now take turns to give your lectures. Your classmates will play the roles of students. While listening to each other, use the checklist below to prepare comments and feedback.

	Yes	No	Comments
1 Is the beginning of the lecture engaging?			
2 As a learner • do you feel involved? • can you follow the lecture easily? • do you understand what's expected from you?			
3 Does the speaker use appropriate classroom English?			

17 Give feedback to each other. Think about the questions below.

- What made you feel involved? (E.g. a question, a metaphor.)
- What can you advise your classmate to do for further development? (E.g. make more eye contact, speak a bit louder.)

Module wrapping-up

1 You have finished Module 3. Congratulations! Reflect on the module and evaluate your progress. Read the statements in the table below and tick them if you agree with them.

Module 3	
I can present my academic profile in English.	
I can write a syllabus in English.	
I can structure and deliver a class in English.	
I can use classroom English in teaching my subject matter.	
I can participate in discussions in English.	

2 What do you need to improve further? Set yourself some goals for further development. Use the SMART principle: goals should be Specific, Measurable, Achievable, Realistic, Time-bound.

3 Share your responses to the module with the whole class.

Leading a discussion

Module 3, Unit 1, Lesson 2

1 Read the guidelines and the Language Support box below.

Guidelines for a discussion leader

1 Start and conclude the discussion, paying attention to the agreed time limits.

2 Give all group members an equal chance to participate. You may have to control those who talk too much and to involve quiet participants.

3 Make sure that all group members can understand each other. You may have to ask people to speak more slowly or loudly so that everyone can understand them.

4 Keep the discussion moving. You may have to refocus the discussion politely if members spend too much time on one point or start repeating the same ideas. However, you also have to decide when it is useful to allow the discussion to flow.

5 Keep the discussion on the subject. If participants move on to a completely different subject or start bringing up irrelevant points, you should politely bring the discussion back to the subject.

2 Take notes during the discussion.

3 Be ready to summarise the information of the group discussion and present the summary to the whole class.

Language Support: leading a discussion

Getting started
Is everybody ready to begin?
OK. Are we ready to start?

Encouraging everyone to participate
What do you think about (*name*)'s point?
Does anyone have anything to add?
Would anyone like to comment on what (*name*) said?

Controlling people who talk too much
Let's hear what some others have to say.
I think you've got a good point there. Why don't we find out what other people think?

Keeping the discussion moving
Perhaps we should go on to the next point.
We have only a few minutes left, so could we move on?
Are there any more comments before we move on to the next point?

Keeping the discussion on the subject
That's interesting, but it raises a different point. Could we come back to that later?

Summing up
So, to sum up, we've discussed ...

Academic vocabulary

Conferences and seminars

announcement
call for papers
chairperson
checklist
deadline
facilitate/facilitator
facilities
feedback
moderate/moderator
panel discussion
panellist
participant
plenary
poster presentation
proposal
question-and-answer (Q&A) session
register/registration
round table (discussion)
session
timeline
venue
workshop

Writing for publication

abstract
annotated bibliography
chapter
citation
consider for publication
contribute/contributor
criterion (plural: criteria)
editor/editorial board
evaluation (critical evaluation)
evidence
footnote
guidelines for authors
investigation (= research)
limitation (of research)
manuscript
peer-reviewed article/journal
proof-reading
quantitative or qualitative methods
rationale
refereed journal
reference
reject
replicate (an experiment)
revise/revision
research gap
review (book review, literature review)
sample
scope
speculation
submission
survey
validity

Course types and delivery modes

bachelor's degree programme
blended learning
crowd learning
degree
distance education/learning
fieldwork
flipped classroom
geo-learning
joint course
joint/dual degree
laboratory session
lecture
master's degree programme
MOOC (massive open online course)
multi-layered instruction
presentation
seamless learning
self-directed learning
seminar
tutorial
workshop

Processes in higher education

accept/acceptance
accomplish/accomplishment
achieve/achievement
analyse/analysis
apply/application
appoint/appointment
assess/assessment
assign/assignment
assume/assumption
attend/attendance
categorise/categorisation
clarify/clarification
collaborate/collaboration
comprehend/comprehension
contribute/contribution
define/definition
deliver/delivery
demonstrate/demonstration
design (verb and noun)
develop/development
discuss/discussion
engage/engagement
enrol/enrolment
evaluate/evaluation
facilitate/facilitation
generalise/generalisation
innovate/innovation
integrate/integration
internationalise/internationalisation
interpret/interpretation
introduce/introduction
investigate/investigation
involve/involvement
motivate/motivation
observe/observation
participate/participation
partner (verb and noun)/partnership
perform/performance
predict/prediction
present/presentation
progress/progression
publish/publication
qualify/qualification
rank/ranking
reflect/reflection
reject/rejection
register/registration
require/requirement
research (verb and noun)
review (verb and noun)
summarise/summary
survey (verb and noun)
synthesise/synthesis
validate/validation

Curriculum, assessment and evaluation

aim
assignment
computer-based testing/assessment
continuous assessment
credit/credit rating/credit-bearing
criterion (plural: criteria)
essay
formative assessment
goal
grade/grading
mark (verb and noun)
method of assessment
multiple-choice question/test
objective (noun)
objective/subjective assessment
outcome/learning outcome
portfolio
quiz
set a test/task/assignment
summative assessment
syllabus/syllabus design
template
term paper (AmE)
test (verb and noun)

Teaching techniques and support for teaching

anecdote
background reading

content (noun)

critical thinking/promote critical thinking

debate

flowchart

handout

ice-breaker/break the ice

input

make notes

mnemonic

motivate

project

rapport/build rapport

review

revise

simulation

task

technique

trigger interest

visual

Useful combinations with verbs

accept/reject a hypothesis/a proposal/an article

attend a course/class/lecture/seminar

build rapport

chair a panel/discussion/debate

clarify a concept/question

design materials/a course/a syllabus/a curriculum/a programme/an experiment

draw a conclusion

form a partnership/hypothesis

hold an appointment/a position/a qualification/a degree (in)

host a conference/website/forum/round table/dinner

make a contribution/a suggestion/a proposal/an application/an assumption/notes

master a skill

meet expectations/objectives

post something online

provide/offer evidence

review progress/a proposal/an article/a book

set a test/an assignment

Acknowledgements

The British Council would like to express sincere gratitude to the authors of the book for their dedication and professionalism.

Svetlana Bogolepova, NRU Higher School of Economics, Moscow
Vasiliy Gorbachev, British Higher School of Art and Design, Moscow
Olga Groza, Siberian Federal University, Krasnoyarsk
Anisya Ivanova, Siberian Federal University, Krasnoyarsk
Lyudmila Kuznetsova, St Petersburg State University, Saint-Petersburg
Tamara Oschepkova, Omsk State Pedagogical University, Omsk
Irina Pervukhina, Ural State University of Economics, Ekaterinburg
Ekaterina Shadrova, Vologda State University, Vologda
Svetlana Suchkova, Samara State Aerospace University, Samara

The British Council and the authors would also like to extend its gratitude to the project consultant, Rod Bolitho without whose unfailing support, commitment and expertise this book would not be possible.

The British Council would also like to thank all Cambridge University editors and other staff who were involved in the process of the book's production.

The authors and publishers acknowledge the following sources of copyright material and are grateful for the permissions granted. While every effort has been made, it has not always been possible to identify the sources of all the material used, or to trace all copyright holders. If any omissions are brought to our notice, we will be happy to include the appropriate acknowledgements on reprinting.

Thomas L. Benson for the text on pp. 48-49 adapted from 'Five Arguments Against Interdisciplinary Studies,' *Issues in Integrative Studies*, 1982. Reproduced with permission;

Cambridge University Press for the text on p. 55 from 'Instructions for Contributors, *Network Science*. Network Science © Cambridge University Press, reproduced with permission;

Cambridge University Press for the text on p. 56 from 'Instructions for Contributors, *Geological Magazine*. Geological Magazine © Cambridge University Press, reproduced with permission;

Fiona Lyddy for the text on pp. 60, 86 adapted from 'Media representation of depression in young people: a corpus-based analysis of Irish newspaper coverage,' by G. Tobin and F. Lyddy, *Irish Journal of Psychological Medicine*, Volume 31, Issue 01, pp. 21–30, 2014 © College of Psychiatrists of Ireland, published by Cambridge University Press, reproduced with permission;

Kieng Tan for the text on pp. 63, 79, 81, 93–94 adapted from 'Encouraging reflection: Do professional development workshops increase the skill level and use of reflection in practice?' by Kieng Tan, Angela Cashell and Amanda Bolderston, *Journal of Radiotherapy* in Practice, Volume 11, Issue 03, pp. 135–144, 2012 © Cambridge University Press, reproduced with permission;

Mariana Szabó for the text on pp. 64, 88, 100 from 'Uncontrolled, Repetitive Eating of Small Amounts of Food or 'Grazing': Development and Evaluation of a New Measure of Atypical Eating' by Brigitte Land and Marianna Szabó, *Behaviour Change*, Volume 30, Issue 02, pp. 57–73 © The Authors 2013, reproduced with permission;

Taylor & Francis / Routledge for the text on pp. 68–69 from 'Learning and talent development,' by Sue Williams *Action Learning Research and Practice*, 21.11.11;

American Sociological Association for the text on p. 70 from 'Book review of 'Families in Today's World: A Comparative Approach' by David Cheal,' by Pamela Ray Koch and Debra H. Swanson, *Teaching Sociology*, Volume 37, No. 3, pp. 324–325, 2009;

Atholl Murray and Zoe J. Hazelwood for the text on pp. 74, 80, 82, 89, 96, 101 from ' Being Grateful: Does It Bring Us Closer Gratitude Attachment and Intimacy in Romantic Relationships' by Atholl J. Murray and Ze J. Hazelwood, *Journal of Relationships*, Volume 2, Issue 1, pp. 17–25, 2011 © Cambridge University Press, reproduced with permission;

The American Society for Cell Biology for the text on p. 91 from 'Teach More by Lecturing Less' by Jennifer K. Knight and William B. Wood, *Cell Biology Education*, Volume 4, Winter 2005, pp. 298–310;

HarperCollins Publishers for the text on p. 86 excerpted from *Physics and Philosophy: The Revolution in Modern Science* by Werner Heisenberg. Copyright © 1958 by Werner Heisenberg. Reprinted by permission of HarperCollins Publishers;

UK Higher Education International Unit for the text on pp. 108–110 adapted from 'Horizon Scanning: What Will Higher Education look like in 2020?" by The Observatory on Borderless Higher Education, September 2013;

Text on p. 113 adapted from 'Pros and Cons of Technology in Education' 19.11.11;

Text on p. 114 adapted from 'Open University Innovation Report 2' by Mike Sharples, Patrick McAndrew, Martin Weller, Rebecca Ferguson, Elizabeth Fitzgerald, Tony Hirst, and Mark Gaved, 2014 © The Open University and https://www.futurelearn.com;

Text on p. 118 from Kiril Larin, Ph.D. faculty profile page, University of Houston, Biomedical Engineering;

Text on p. 119 from About Me, peterjaniszewski.com;

David Robinson for text on p. 137–138 from 'Introduction to Ecosystems Course Description and Web Science', The Open University and https://www.futurelearn.com. Reproduced with permission;

Christian Jarrett for the text on p. 148 from 'Lecturers should provide PowerPoint handouts before the lecture', Research Digest, 7.7.10, The British Psychological Society. Reproduced with permission.

The publisher has used its best endeavours to ensure that the URLs for external websites referred to in this book are correct and active at the time of going to press. However, the publisher has no responsibility for the websites and can make no guarantee that a site will remain live or that the content is or will remain appropriate.

The publishers would like to thank the following illustrators:

Kamae Design: p. 95
Roger Penwill: pp. 23, 61, 69, 92, 101, 144, 157
Sean (KJA artists): pp. 56, 159